THE VEIL LIFTED
FOR THE CURIOUS

OR

THE SECRET OF THE
REVOLUTION IN FRANCE

REVALED WITH THE AID OF FREEMASONRY

by

Jacques-François Lefranc

London
Spradabach Publishing
2022

SPRADABACH PUBLISHING
BM Box Spradabach
London WC1N 3XX

Originally published in French as
*Le Voile levé pour les curieux, ou Le Secret de la Révolution
révélé à l'aide de la Franc-Maçonnerie* in 1791.

Translated by Alex Kurtagic

First English edition published 2022
© Spradabach Publishing 2022

Interior designed by Alex Kurtagic

ISBN 978-1-909606-26-5

British Library Cataloguing-in-Publication Data:
A catalogue record for this book is available from the British Library.

Table of Contents

TABLE OF CONTENTS

Note on this Edition

he present edition is based on the text of the second French edition, published in Paris by Crappat in 1792. The entirety of that text is presented here in English for the first time. The punctuation has been left unchanged, except in a handful of places where the addition or deletion of a comma was thought to improve clarity and flow. The Italics are as in the original, except for book titles referred to in the text, where they have appeared in roman letters. The capitalisation follows the original, except the pronouns relating to Jesus Christ have been capitalised for added clarity. A number of quotation marks where added in Chapter VI, where they appeared to be missing in the original.

A complement of footnotes have been added, providing bibliographical information or context where it was deemed useful. Also added has been a full index.

Introduction

lthough several Authors have attempted to give us a history of Freemasonry, we can say that no one has yet fully informed us of the true nature of this society. I have *read the origin of Freemasonry*[1] *by Mr. Guillemain de Saint-Victor; the order of the Freemasons betrayed; the secret of the mopses revealed;*[2] *the*

---

1   Louis Guillemain de Saint-Victor, *Origine de la maçonnerie adonhiramite: ou Nouvelles observations, critiques et raisonnées, sur la philosophie, les hiéroglyphes, les mysteres, la superstition & les vices des mages* (Hélopolis [Paris], 1787).

2   Gabriel-Louis Pérau, *L'Ordre des francs-maçons trahi et le secret des Mopses révélé* (Amsterdam, 1758).

crushed Freemasons;[3] *the history of Freemasons of Great Britain; the secret of the Freemasons;*[4] *the freemason in the republic;*[5] *the reception mystery of the members of the famous society of freemasons;*[6] *the apologetic and historic relationship as, containing the order and establishment of the Society of Freemasons;*[7] *the obligations of a Freemason;*[8] *the anti-mason;*[9] *the secret of the freemasons hightlighted;*[10] *the apology for the order*

3   Gabriel-Louis Pérau, *Les Francs-Maçons écrasés*. (Amsterdam, 1747).

4   Joseph Uriot, *Le secret des francs-maçons mis en évidence* (The Hague, J. Antoine Barrau, 1744).

5   Philipp F. Steinheil, *Le Franc-maçon dans la république* (Frankfurt and Leipzig, 1746).

6   Samuel Prichard, *La Réception mystérieuse des membres de la célèbre société des francs-maçons* (London: Compagnie des libraires, 1738).

7   *La Relation apologétique et historique, contenant l'ordre et l'établissement de la société des francs-maçons* (London, 1738).

8   James Anderson, *The Constitutions of the Free-Masons. Containing the History, Charges, Regulations, &c. of that Most Ancient and Right Worshipful Fraternity* (London: William Hunter, 1723)

9   *L'Anti-maçon ou Les mystères de la maçonnerie dévoilés par un profane. Augmenté de l'usage des signes, de la manière d'écrire en franc-maçon, & de plusieurs autres usages propres à la Maçonnerie, par le moyen desquels un profane peut passer pour franc-maçon. Avec une lettre d'un franc-maçon à un frere nouvellement reçû* (1748).

10   Joseph Uriot, *Le secret des francs-maçons mis en évidence* (The Hague, J. Antoine Barrau, 1744).

of the Freemasons;[11] *apologetic defense of Freemasons;*[12] *the perfect mason;*[13] *the Catechism of Freemasons;*[14] *Adoniramite masonry; the testament of a freemason;*[15] *Essay on Freemasonry.*[16] *One can add to it the persecuted Freemasons; new dictionary of freemasons; the declamations against Freemasonry, and in general the poems, comedies, and songs made on the subject, and* I dare assure you that we will still not have a clear or true idea of Freemasonry.

Everything is a mystery, an emblem, and a secret in this *royal art*, and the real secret escapes amid simulated secrets, in which all ceremonies are wrapped. There are few Masons there in a po-

---

11 Pierre-Jean-Baptiste Nougaret, *Apologie pour l'ordre des francs-maçons* (The Hague: Pierre Grosse, 1744).

12 *Défense apologetique des francs-maçons* (Frankfurt: Rudolf Fisscher, 1747).

13 *Le Parfait maçon, ou Les Veritables secrets des quatre grades d'Apprentifs, Compagnons, Maîtres ordinaires & Ecossois de la Franche-maçonnerie* (1744).

14 Louis Travenol, *Catechisme Des Francs-Maçons, Précédé d'un Abrégé de l'Histoire d'Adoniram, Architecte du Temple de Salomon, & d'une Explication des Cérémonies qui s'observent à la Reception des Maîtres; le Signe, le Mot & l'Attouchement, qui les distinguent d'avec les Apprentifs Compagnons. Dedié Au Beau Sexe* (Jerusalem and Limoges: Pierre Mortier, 1744).

15 *The Testament of a Freemason, ou Le Testament du Chevalier Graaff* (Brussels, 1745).

16 *Essai sur la franc-maçonnerie, ou du but essentiel et fondamental de la F. M. de la possibilité et de la necessité de la réunion des différents systêmes our branches de la M.; du régime convenable à ces systêmes réunis, & des loix Maç.* (Paris: Xiste Andron, 1784).

sition to discover the truth, although they are assured that it is found only in a lodge, and that it is veiled from the eyes of the profane. However, since today it is, more than ever, interesting for those who are Masons, and for those who are not but who can become, to see in what this order consists, and for what it has been established, we will examine the mystery of its origin, its ceremonies, its purpose, and the commitments which a person contracts upon entering it; it's from all this that we hope to bring out a great light, more interesting and brighter than that which shines in the astonished eyes of a young Mason. The latter hits and dazzles but the eyes of the body; the former, by contrast, will enlighten his soul, and will uncover before him a sinister project, the consummation of its intent's most criminal iniquity, and the most dangerous that has yet manifested to the world since the origin of Christianity.

CHAPTER I

The Origin of Freemasonry

The more the Freemasons have made a mystery of their origin, the more we have sought to discover it. In this respect, each of them has claimed to have the secret, and yet this is known to few people. All the speeches that the orators make in the lodge on the origin, the progress of the royal art of masonry, either say nothing essential, or tend only to mislead the curious. Printed books, both in verse and in prose, substitute real masonry for moral masonry; and confound the origin of one with that of the other, interchanging it continuously to unreflecting readers. True Masons, in the sense of Freemasonry, build temples to virtue, and dungeons to vices; but have never erected a public monument: however, to give themselves an antique air that garners them respect, the masons associate themselves with all those who by some memorable work distinguished themselves in antiquity, such as Hiram, Adoniram, Solomon, Noah, Adam; some even do not fear to elevate themseves to God, and to take Him for the master of their art, of which He has taught lessons by forming the vault of the heavens.

They could not trace their origin any higher; and if it were in their power to give us a history from the beginning of the world to the present day, there is no doubt that the society of the Freemasons would be the most respectable and noble body in the world; to which it would not be possible to refuse the first rank, nor to contradict its maxims. But unfortunately not all agree on such a beautiful origin; and however flattering it may be as a whole, and for each individual in particular, we are obliged, for lack of authentic memoirs, to bring it closer to our time, from which it is not far removed, if we believe the truth of history.

Some Freemasons claim to fix their first beginnings at the time of the Crusades, when the Europeans rebuilt the cities that they themselves, or the Saracens, had destroyed. But for every answer we can remind these gentlemen that, by their own admission, one should not take the Masons' word in its proper sense, but in a symbolic and figurative sense, and consequently in every other meaning than that which they wish to attach to it. Besides, how would they prove that it is the Society of Masons, of which they are members, which rebuilt the towns of Palestine? Who transmitted to them the memoirs supporting these claims? Nowhere in history is it seen that the Freemasons of today have undertaken a task as useful as it is glorious.

It is true that the Freemasons of England date their origin from the year 924, and consequently from a time prior to that of the Crusades, which is still not in question; but does it prove Freemasonry existed at that time? No, no doubt; because it would follow that Freemasonry would have taken its origin in France, while the French themselves agree that it is in England where it began. The masons whom Adelstant, son of the great Alfred, brought from France to England, were therefore not Freemasons, but architects and working masons, of which he formed a body, to which he gave statutes, and assigned places of assembly. It is true that the Freemasons of England were formed after the example of the Masons of this kingdom; that they gave themselves supervisors, apprentices, servants, masters, fellows of the craft, architects; that they had designated assemblies; that they formed themselves into associations; that they were bound by oaths: but are they for that reason masons? No, they are only its apes; and the resemblance of their corporations in no way proves the resemblance of their origin.

But, you will say to me, they have, like masons, aprons, squares, plumbs, drawing boards, hammers, trowels, compasses: that is true; but the masons erect buildings and temples for the use of the citizens: the Freemasons, on the contrary, wish only to overthrow and destroy them. If they say that they occupy themselves with erecting temples to virtue, and building dungeons to vices, all this must be understood in a moral sense, and does not mean anything else, except that Freemasons flatter themselves with establishing virtue on the ruins of vice. So they are not masons properly so called, according to the natural sense of the name which they attribute to themselves. This is not the time to examine whether the Freemasons have the object of making men more virtuous; we will do so elsewhere.

Some of those who maintain that Freemasonry originated in England go no further back than Cromwell; and the author of the book entitled *Les Francs-Macons écrasés, ou l'Ordre des Francs-Maçons trahi*, is of this sentiment. 'His object,' he said,

> was to build a new edifice, that is to say, to reform the human race, by exterminating the kings and the powers of which this usurper was the scourge. Now, to give his followers a sensible idea of his design, he proposed to them the restoration of the Temple of Salomon . . . . This temple was built by the order that God gave to this prince. It was the sanctuary of re-

ligion, the place specially consecrated to its august ceremonies; it was for the splendour of this temple that this wise monarch had established so many ministers charged with watching over its purity and its embellishment. Finally, after several years of glory and magnificence, comes a formidable army which overthrows this illustrious monument. The people, who there rendered their homage to the Divinity, are put in irons and conducted to Babylon, whence, after the most rigorous captivity, they were released by the hand of their God. An idolatrous prince, chosen to be the instrument of divine mercy, allows this unfortunate people, not only to rebuild the temple in its first splendour, but also to take advantage of the means that he provides to succeed in it.

Now, it is in this allegory that the Freemasons find the exact resemblance of their society. This temple, they say, considered in its first luster, is the figure of the primitive state in which man emerges from nothingness. This religion, these ceremonies that are practised, are nothing other than that common law, engraved in all hearts, which finds its principle in the ideas of equity and charity, to which men are obliged among themselves. The destruction of this temple, the enslavement of its worshippers, those are pride and ambition, that have introduced dependence among men. The Assyrians, that pitiless army, those are the kings, the princes, the magistrates whose power has caused so much misfortune as to oppress men; finally this chosen people, responsible for restoring this magnificent temple, are the Freemasons, who must give back to the universe its first beauty.

I believe that the Freemasons have been able to make similar remarks, and even more extravagant ones, because they believe themselves made to reform the human race, but I will not agree as readily on Freemasonry owing its origin to Cromwell, nor on this great protector of England having the project of founding a new religion and making himself its chief. Those who knew him best never attributed such sentiments to him. A profound politician, he limited his ambition to making good use of the authority and power which he had been able to gather on his head. He seemed to play at religion by the skill with which he moved, according to his views, the different sects who then divided England by their opinions. He never adopted any out of taste or in good faith; and it is wrong to impute him with having wished to form a system of irreligion or to draw up the plan of the society of Freemasons.

We can assure the reader that quite far from being certain that Cromwell wanted to found the society of Freemasons, it has been demonstrated that it originated not in England. Those who have reasoned most accurately on its origin, have it come from the North. It is, in fact, from the northern countries that it passed towards the south, and that it then spread into all the countries of the inhabited world.

The time of its existence does not go back, as Mr. Guillemain de Saint-Victor claims, to the fabulous times of Egypt, nor to the mysteries of Eleusis or Isis. It was only in France that we have given to

Freemasonry such an extravagant origin, to confuse all those who would follow the progress and growth of this society; but this air of erudition and antiquity we wanted to lend to it has had no luck with true scholars, and has only really been able obtrude itself among the ignorant.

It is among them also that the false Count of Cagliostro made fools and grew rich. He borrowed some of the scholarly and enigmatic features paraded by M. Guillemain de Saint-Victor; he invented new tests, affected to possess the science of nature, to have discovered singular and extraordinary remedies, to have found the philosopher's stone. With such secrets he travelled throughout Europe, and acquired a great reputation, which he abused whenever he found occasion.

But there is nothing in the Freemasonry invented by Cagliostro that is not indicated in the trials which M. Guillemain claims were observed in Memphis, at the initiation of the priests of Isis. Part of it was rehearsed in Paris, in the lodge of the Faubourg Saint-Antoine, at the Hôtel de la Nouvelle France; we can see them in full in the work entitled: *On the Origin of Freemasonry.* They are able, effectively, to make tenable anything observed in the ordinary lodges, the more difficult and the more extraordinary, because they imitate but very remotely what must have been practiced in Egypt during the initiations of new candidates.

One of the advantages Freemasons have drawn from the so-called Egyptian initiation is to have lent some verisimilitude to the creation of the offices they have established in their lodges. You cannot be admitted unless you have a sponsor, that is to say, someone who introduces you, to enter the lodge; and to lend greater eminence to the one in charge of having you admitted to the number of initiates, they take care to relate to you what was done in Egypt, accompanying it with mysterious precautions, as if the entrance to the lodge was the holiest thing imaginable.

'It is strictly prohibited,' says M. Guillemain,

> to the initiates to invite anyone to be received among them. When a man, of whatever rank, went to ask for initiation, the priests affected to grant it to him with ease; but at the same time they made him write down his name and his application, and assigned him an initiate to inform him of his trials. The latter took care to learn about the morals and the religion, the country of origin and the quality of the candidate, and warned him that it was absolutely necessary that an initiate answer to him, lest he gives himself away or become complacent.

To justify the inquisition that they make in Freemasonry, of the morals, of the religion, of the character, of the wealth of a candidate, care is taken to tell him:

> that this formality was observed by everyone in their initiation into the ancient mysteries; that Hercules even had to be adopted by an initiated

Athenian when he wanted to be initiated into Athens. M. Guillemain even goes so far as to name his sponsor, who was called *Pylas*, and this generic term means sponsor, according to these learned scholars.

Wouldn't you say that by entering Freemasonry, one becomes another man? The initiation, says M. Guillemain, is the end of profane life, regarded as animal life: that means, that by being initiated into the mysteries of Masonry, one passes from the coarse and animal life, to a spiritual and almost supernatural life: this is the baptism of Masons:

> it is a death to vice; the love of virtue and of duties takes the place of all the passions in him who receives this initiation; his being, or rather the principle that animates it, is renewed. This is the effect of baptism among Christians; but it is not produced by the same principle. Yes, without a doubt, adds our doctor, to substitute knowledge and virtues for ignorance and prejudice is to drive the soul into another body.

Such is the idea that our Masons form of metempsychosis, so common among the ancients; but as they have all religion consist of morality, we cannot reflect too much on the principles following, about which we read from the same author.

"The initiate," he says,

> must reflect on his existence, be accountable for his intentions and actions; to be always on

guard against himself, and work unceasingly to
perfect himself: he must pity the foolish, and try
to instruct them; to flee the wicked, to succour
the unfortunate, to put among the number of
human weaknesses pride, covetousness, envy:
in whatever rank he finds himself placed by
birth or fortune, he should believe himself established there only to be useful, and to do good
for humanity in general; finally, he must study
nature, respect what he cannot fathom, and im-
bue his soul with the most sublime truths.

This morality and these principles might suit
pagans who had no knowledge of a supernatural life; but that Masons who have been baptised
adopt them and teach them as the sole epitome of
their morality, that is what many people will find
hard to believe; they are very unhappy if the greatest effort of their reason, aided by all the light they
have received from revelation, makes them return
to the point from which the pagan philosophers set
out to discover: the principles on which morality is
founded!

To justify the laws prescribed to Freemasons in
the lodges, which are: to write the catechism of the
degrees they have received, to make oaths, to keep
an inviolable secret on all that happens in the lodge,
Mr. Guillemain takes care to observe that all these
practices were in use in the ancient mysteries.

'The laws of the candidate,' he said,

required that each write down the morals and
the object which he proposed to have as a ba-

sis for all the actions of his life; his consent to
fulfil, with the greatest exactitude, all the duties
which initiation would impose on him; that he
would take an oath, in the presence of the gods
and the priests, to keep inviolably secret all the
mysteries which were revealed to him, or which
he saw practiced. He was warned that he must
think carefully about all these articles, so as not
to write anything against the feelings and inten-
tions of his heart.

Could M. Guillemain answer us regarding the
freedom which a candidate enjoys in the midst
of the frightful ordeals through which he is made
to pass? And when his freedom is indisputable,
what does the new morality that they want him to
swear mean? If it is superior to that of the Gospel,
I will ask him where the Freemasons got it; if it is
inferior or contrary to it, let him tell us why it is
proposed to candidates, if it is not to make them
forget the great principles of perfection which
we hold from *Jesus Christ*, the law-giver of the
Christians. In order to motivate the seriousness
and silence which are prescribed for candidates
in Masonry, great care was taken to quote what
was required of candidates who were admitted to
the mysteries.

'The candidate,' continues our author,

> was abandoned to his own reflections for some
> time; then they led him into a dark dome, lit
> by a single lamp and located at the back of the
> sanctuary, and they left him in the hands of ei-

ther his handler or his sponsor. (This is how the sponsor leads the apprentice Freemason into a dark chamber lit by the dim light of a lamp.) The latter, accompanied by a priest, called Hydranos, who acted as the Terrible brother, asked the candidate: whether of all the trials he had undergone, none seemed to him ridiculous and superfluous? Whether he had really decided to receive the initiation, and to respect it even in the smallest circumstances?

When the candidate answered in conformity with what was required of him, the Hydranos made him strip naked to the waist, brought him near a basin filled with water from the sea or from the Nile, to which had been added salt, barley, and bay leaf; he then ordered him to put his hands in the basin, and poured water on his head (as observed in Masonry), saying: 'May this water, symbol of purity, erase all that may have defiled your flesh; and by restoring to you your candour and your first innocence, purify your body: as virtue must purify your soul.' These words finished, he dressed the candidate in a fine linen jacket or dress.

In Masonry, they provide a shirt and underpants, declaring that those who have received the new baptism, *in derision of that of Christians*, are pure and innocent. Those who have not received it are regarded as profane, unworthy to participate in the mysteries of Masonry. The ceremonies observed in the lodge after the first trials are still modelled on those supposed to have been practiced among the ancients.

The day of initiation was called new *regeneration*; it was celebrated by feasts. Apuleius expresses himself thus: 'I had a coat of fine linen striped with white, blue, purple, and scarlet; crowned with palm branches, I was shown to the people. They then celebrated my new birth with a feast.'

It was necessary, without doubt, that the meal which follows the reception of a Freemason, should still be dictated by an ancient custom, in order to render more plausible the conformity which they claim to establish between the mysteries of paganism, and those of Masonic lodges. But as the meals which are taken in the lodge are gay, and accompanied by pleasant jokes, great care is taken to justify them by what was practiced at the initiations of Athens. Let us resume the story of Apuleius.

After that, the initiate was taken to the dome, where symbolic requests were made to him, to which he responded according to what he had been taught. After which, the candidate was introduced into the sanctuary of the temple in the midst of the deepest darkness; the horror was increased by all that human industry can imagine of the terrible. Thunder rumbles from all sides, lightning bolts, lightning strikes, the air is filled with monstrous figures, the sanctuary trembles, and if the earth seems to open up. But soon the calm succeeds the storm, and to the crash of the unleashed elements, the scene unfolds and extends into the distance, the bottom of the sanctuary opens, and one sees a pleasant meadow, where he goes to rejoice.

Pure and innocent pleasures are the only hopes which a Freemason should flatter himself with enjoying. This is what they want him to understand by what follows:

> An open and comfortable temple, built in a pleasant and rural garden, surrounded and shaded by trees whose branches seemed to be lost in the clouds, was the place where the initiate was introduced.

Here is the dogma and the morality that ministers of religion must content themselves with teaching with modesty, for fear of making a mistake. This piece is by M. Guillemain and reveals all his feelings.

> The eyes of the new proselyte were not hurt by the material and ridiculous representations of the gods imagined by men. The brilliant star which lights up all mortals, the sky, with a pure and tranquil light, was what presented itself to his gaze when he raised it. The Magi, dressed uniformly, arranged in a semicircle (*as they do in the lodge*), having their disciples in their midst, seemed to blush at the pride and presumption they had shown so far. One could read in their demeanour and in their looks, that they sought only to speak like modest sages, who tremble at making a mistake in desiring to instruct.

He whom all the others regarded as a scholar, began by proving that there is a unique and supreme God, the mover and preserver of the universe. He demonstrated, by deep reasoning, that matter could not acquire, by itself, motion and intelligence. He confessed that those who were regarded as demi-gods had only been men celebrated for their wisdom and knowledge, whom the course of time had deified in the minds of the people; but let the priests and initiates content themselves with honouring their memory, and imitating their virtues; that, finally, the respect they had for them was only that which one owes to enlightened legislators, such as those who were the founders of Egyptian glory.

'According to these truths,' said the orator, 'it will perhaps be difficult for you to understand the motive which makes us act so contradictorily in civil society. We groan in secret to profane the Divinity by illusions and lies; but we have the weakness to believe that the people, who live in ignorance, need images which can be perceived by their senses. We believe they incapable of adoring an impassive being whom they cannot understand.'

If the Magi and the Ministers of Religion, who had the secret of the mysteries of the Egyptians, had really given these instructions to those who let themselves be initiated into their mysteries, M. Guillemain is asked why the Egyptians passed, among all peoples, as the most superstitious of all men? Why, in the time of Plutarch, was it unknown that there was, among the Egyptians, religious instructions made for reasonable people, and others for ignorant and rude people? For, in the judgment of this contemporary author, the Egyptians adored not only the ibis and the ichneumon, which were useful animals; but also the crocodile, which ate men; 'which rendered them ridiculous to foreigners, and exposed,' says Plutarch,

> the worship and ceremonies of religion to the contempt and ridicule of reasonable people; gave occasion to the most absurd ideas and the most detestable actions; produced, in feeble minds, the most extravagant superstition; plunged strong minds into the horrors of atheism, or at least they led to impious opinions which degraded humanity so much that Divinity itself found itself degraded by the worship of animals.' (Leland's *Démonstration évangélique*).

These, according to M. Guillemain, are the ones Freemasons should take as a model: would it remind us of atheism or idolatry; to make us ridiculous to foreigners, and to make us relapse into the absurdities for which the ancient philosophers are rightly reproached? What is certain, it is that in wishing to describe to us the ceremonies used in the mysteries of Isis or Ceres, he surely has not given us the origin of Freemasonry; and if we had to believe him on his word, there would be nothing very flattering for the great order he wants to celebrate, since it would follow, from his discoveries, that Freemasonry took its source from the centre of idolatry, and recalls there those who are initiated into its mysteries. If this is where all the efforts of the new philosophy lead, if those who do not want to admit the mysteries of revealed Religion, are obliged to adopt all the reveries of paganism, it must be admitted, the human spirit, left to its own light, is very weak and much to be pitied.

But, let us agree in good faith, not all Freemasons are of Mr. Guillemain's opinion. There are some who trace the origin of Freemasonry to the appearance of *Jesus Christ* on the shores of the Jordan, when the three persons of the Holy Trinity bore witness to his divine mission: it is for this reason that the feast of St John the Baptist is so famous throughout the Masonic order. Some enthusiasts persuade themselves that the first lodge was held in earthly Paradise, when God appeared to Adam and to Eve. Those who belong to high Masonry, and who make a profession of cultivating the abstract sciences, of discovering mysterious knowledge, hidden under allegories and emblems, trace the origin of Masonry to Métraim or Menes, to Thoz, Hermes or Mercury-Trismegistus; others to the Essenes or Esseans; others to Druids or Gomer. It may be said that the philosophers of our day, having borrowed from the schools of ancient philosophy several usages which they have introduced into Masonic lodges, Masonry in some respects looks like whatever we want, and that it is almost impossible to find its true origin.

Freemasons claim to be descended from the Druids, because they recognise, like them, the Supreme Being, whom they honour; they forbid, like them, to discuss matters of religion and politics; they impose secrecy on the dogmas they want to hide from outsiders; they respect, like them, the dead, keeping their skulls to drink from, a practice that Freemasons observe, above all with respect to the skull of Adoniram, their Grand Master; because they write down nothing concerning their doctrine; they witness the sunrise on the days of Ceremony, like the Druids, who were dressed in white to pick the mistletoe; they have feathers in their hat, like the great Druid priest wore in his cap.

The Freemasons claim to be descended from the Egyptian priests, because they have, like them, a double doctrine, one outward and the other inward. They imitate, in their lodges, the silence that Pythagoras required of his disciples; and, in their degrees, the tests that this philosopher required of his disciples before allowing them to speak. The mystery of their ceremonies, of their sentiments, was represented by the sphinx, which the priests of Isis used to place before the door of their temples. By imitating the usages of all antiquity, and by copying the sentiments of all the philosophers, the Freemasons can truly call themselves cosmopolitans, and trace their origin as far back as they wish.

What we can notice, in all their researches, is that they affect never to speak of the Christian Religion, nor of its morals, nor of its dogmas, nor of the heroic virtues that it orders or that it advises, although she alone has produced more virtues, enlightenment, and happiness, than all human institutions together. But the object of Freemasonry is not to offer *Jesus Christ* as a model, nor to take lessons from Him. It is fitting that, following in the footsteps of Socinus, its founder, it should work to erase, if possible, His name from the hearts of all Christians.

Here is another origin given to it by the author of *Essai sur la Franc-maçonnerie*, volume 1, p. 76.

It was, without doubt, when the priesthood and the magistracy were united in the same head, that Freemasonry must have been born. The sciences and the principles of the arts were not known but by the *priest-magistrate*. The mechanics of the arts was in the hands of ordinary men. It was necessary, for the happiness of men and their unity, to regulate their morals, and they were given precepts, orders, laws; penalties were inflicted on them; the religion they were taught was brought within their understanding. When the Supreme Being created man, he created all that exists; and at that moment shone, for man, the true light, the light of divine wisdom. Freemasonry has as its era that of the creation of the universe, the era of the true lodge. The study of the sciences and intellectual knowledge, those by which one reads in the fibres of plants, in the bowels of the earth, in the abyss of the seas, in the fire of the stars and planets, in the soul of the man, in the soul of the universe; this study was the priest-magistrate's occupation, and the fruit of this study was gathered by other men, to whose happiness it was destined. Beyond the two doctrines, one which, by its sublimity or its complexity, could not be understood by the common man, and the other which, by its simplicity, was within his reach, the magistracy being separated from the priesthood, intellectual knowledge and that of the sciences were divided; both suffered from the split in their unity; the tree *became sterile* and no longer bore fruit, the tree languished and went into decline. The book of knowledge was written in hieroglyphic characters, in emblems; the secret of these characters was lost, and the imagination, working on the hieroglyphics, became heated, exalted, and saw what was not there, and did not see what was there. By dint of studies and research, they discovered some traces of knowledge; but they were isolated men who sought the light, the truth. They worked alone, they did not communicate their discoveries to each other, and the progress was overwhelmingly slow. *Freemasonry* rose from the tomb; it was seen rising from its ashes like the phoenix; everything that was mysterious was believed to belong to *Freemasonry*; and it was true. All abstract sciences, supernatural knowledge, were grafted onto the Masonic tree. They were detached branches that were grafted onto the trunk. They took the branches for the trunk of the tree: man does not always see clearly. Systems were born, and we saw many of them. The partisans of these systems tore off Free-masonry for themselves and pretended that it belonged exclusively to them. They did not see that it was their systems which belonged to Freemasonry. I repeat it, and I say it, as I believe it, all that is mysterious is the province of Freemasonry; all that is called physical, mental, spiritual, or intellectual knowledge, is the responsibility of Freemasonry and belongs to it; all that can tend to the physical, moral, or intellectual happiness of man, comes from Freemasonry and belongs to it. (See *Essai sur la franc-maçonnerie, ou but essentielet fondamental de la maçonnerie; de la possibilité de la réunion, des différens systêmes de la maçonnerie; du régime convenable à ces systèmes.*) But those who pretend to raise a new temple to the Lord, recognise in King Solomon the head of all Masonic workers, and all Masonic ceremonies and institutions go back to him. Little curious to find the true origin of such a famous order, the Masons gladly leave their members free to choose such origin as they wish to adopt, provided that a thick veil covers the true beginnings of the royal art of Masonry. But in order not to leave the reader in suspense any longer, we will begin to reveal the great, the true, the only secret of Freemasonry, concerning which all Masons have bewildered any who wanted to know it.

Freemasonry is the quintessence of all the heresies which divided Germany in the sixteenth century. The Lutherans, the Calvinists, the Zwinglians, the Anabaptists, the new Arians, all those, in a word, who attack the mysteries of revealed Religion, all those who dispute *Jesus Christ*'s divinity, the Blessed Virgin's divine motherhood; all those who do not recognize the authority of the Catholic Church, or who reject the sacraments; those who do not hope for an afterlife; who do not believe in God, either because they persuade themselves that he does not meddle in the things of this world, or because they wish there were none; these were the ones who gave birth to Freemasonry, or with whom the Freemasons associated themselves, and of whom their royal order is today composed. The proof will be easily grasped by all who possess the history of the end times. We are going to make a few comparisons which will help those who do not have historical books at their fingertips to find the thread which will suffice for them to get out of the labyrinth within which they have been skilfully ensnared.

It is from England that the Freemasons of France claim to derive their origin; it is therefore among our neighbours that we must examine the progress of Masonry. There was no question regarding them at the beginning of the last century. In was in the middle of it that they suffered, under the reign of Cromwell, because they incorporated themselves with the Independents, who then formed a great party. After the death of the Lord Protector, their reputation declined, and it was only towards the end of the seventeenth century that they succeeded in forming separate assemblies, under the name of Freemasons, free men, or free masons; and they were only known in France and only succeeded in gaining proselytes there by means of the English and the Irish, who passed into that kingdom with King James and the Pretender. It was among the troops that they were first known, and among them that they gained proselytes, becoming formidable from 1760, with M. de Clermont, abbot of Saint-Germain-des-Prés as their leader.[1]

But we must go back further to obtain the first and true origin of Freemasonry. Vicenza was the cradle of Masonry in 1546. It was in the society of atheists and deists who had assembled there to confer together on the matters of Religion, which divided Germany in a great number of sects and parties, that the foundations of Masonry were laid: it was in this famous academy that the difficulties, which concerned the mysteries of the Christian Religion, were regarded as points of doctrine, which

---

1   Louis, Comte de Clermont (1709 - 1771), the son of Louis de Bourbon, or Louis III, Prince of Condé and Louise Françoise de Bourbon, Mademoiselle de Nantes (1673–1743), a legitimated daughter of Louis XIV, became abbot of Saint-Germain-des-Près in 1743, whenceupon he embarked on a substantial restoration project. By this time he had been enjoying a parallel military career, having obtained permission from Clement VII to bear arms in 1733. In 1743, he succeeded Louis de Pardaillan de Gondrin, duc d'Antin, as Grand Master of all the regular lodges of France—around 20 in Paris as of 1744 and as many in the provinces. The fifth to hold that position, and a future member of the Academie Française, Clermont held it for nearly thirty years. —Ed.

belonged to the philosophy of the Greeks and not to faith.

These decisions had no sooner come to the knowledge of the Republic of Venice, than it caused the authors of them to be prosecuted with the greatest severity. They arrested Jules Trévisan and François de Rugo, who were strangled. Bernardino Ochino, Lælius Socinus, Peruta, Gentilis, Jacques Chiari, François Le Noir, Darius Socinus, Alcias, the Abbé Léonard fled to where they could; and this dispersion was one of the causes which contributed to the spread of their doctrine in different parts of Europe. Lælius Socin, after having made a famous name among the principal leaders of the heretics who set Germany on fire, died at Zurich, with the reputation of having most strongly attacked the truth of the mystery of the Holy Trinity, as well as that of the Incarnation, the existence of original sin, and the necessity of the grace of *Jesus Christ*.

Lælius Socin left in Faustus Socinus, his nephew, a skilful defender of his opinions; and it is to his talents, to his science, to his indefatigable activity, and to the protection of the princes whom he knew how to place in his party, that Freemasonry owes its origin, its first establishments, and the collection of the principles which are the basis of his doctrine.

Faustus Socinus found much opposition to overcome in order to have his doctrine adopted among the German sectarians; but his supple character, his eloquence, his resources, and above all his object of declaring war on the Roman Church and of destroying it, attracted many partisans to him. His successes were so rapid, that although Luther and Calvin had attacked the Roman Church with the most outrageous violence, Socinus far surpassed them. As an epitaph, these two verses have been placed on his tomb at Luclavia:

> *Tota licet Babylon destroyit tecta Lutherus,*
> *Muros Calvinus, sed fundamenta Socinus.*

which mean that if Luther had destroyed the roof of the Catholic Church, designated by the name of Babylon, if Calvin had knocked down its walls, Socinus could boast of having uprooted its very foundations. The exploits of these sectarians against the Roman Church were represented in caricatures as indecent as they were glorious to each party; for it is to be noted that Germany was filled with engravings of all kinds, in which each contested the glory of having done the most harm to the Church.

But it is certain that none of the chiefs of the sectaries conceived a plan so vast, so impious as that formulated by Socinus against the Church; not only did he seek to overthrow and destroy; he undertook more, to raise a new temple, into which he proposed to admit all the sectarians, uniting all the parties, taking in all the errors, by making a monstrous whole of contradictory principles; for he sacrificed everything to the glory of uniting all the sects, to found a new church in place of that of *Jesus Christ*, which he made it a capital point to overthrow, in order to cut off the faith of the Mysteries, the use of the Sacraments, the terrors of another life, so overwhelming for the wicked.

This great project of building a new temple, of founding a new religion, gave rise to the disciples of Socinus arming themselves with aprons, hammers, squares, plumbs, trowels, tracing boards, as if they wanted to make use of it in the building of the new temple that their leader had planned; but in truth, they are only jewels, ornaments that serve as embellishment, rather than useful instruments for building.

His conduct corresponded to his plans. So that his work may progress without obstacles, he prescribed a profound silence on his enterprise, as the Freemasons prescribe it in their lodges, in matters of religion, in order not to experience any contradiction on the explanation of the religious symbols of which their lodges are full, and they make an oath never to speak, in front of the profane, of what happens in the lodge, so as not to divulge a doctrine which can only be perpetuated under a mysterious veil. In order to bind his followers more closely together, Socinus wanted them to treat each other as brothers, and felt likewise. From this came the names which the Socinians bore successively of *frères unis*, of *frères polonois*, of *frères moraves*, of *frey-maurur*, of *frères de la congregation*, of *frée-murer*, of *freys-maçons*, of *frée-maçons*.

Among themselves, they always treat each other as brothers, and have for each other the most demonstrative friendship.

Socinus derived great advantage from the union of all the Anabaptist, Unitarian, and Trinitarian sects, which he knew how to manage. He saw himself master of all the facilities belonging to these sectarians; he had permission to preach and write his doctrine; he wrote catechisms and books, and would have succeeded in perverting in a short time all the Catholics of Poland, had the Diet of Warsaw not put an obstacle in his way. In fact, never was a doctrine more opposed to Catholic dogma than that of Socinus. Like the Unitarians, he rejected all that had the appearance of mysteries in religion; according to him, *Jesus Christ* was only the son of God by adoption and by the prerogatives that God had granted him to be our mediator, our priest, our pontiff, albeit just a man. According to Socinus and the Unitarians, the Holy Spirit is not God; and far from admitting three persons in God, Socinus wanted only one, who was God. He regarded as dreams the mystery of the Incarnation, the real presence of *Jesus Christ* in the Eucharist, the existence of original sin, the necessity of a sanctifying grace. The Sacraments were in his eyes only pure ceremonies established to support the religion of the people. The apostolic Tradition was not, in his eyes, a rule of faith; he did not recognize the authority of the Church to interpret the Holy Scriptures. In a word, the doctrine of Socinus is contained in two hundred and twenty-nine articles, all of which have for their object overturning *Jesus Christ*'s doctrine.

When Socinus died, in 1604, his sect was so well established that it obtained freedom of conscience in the diets of Poland. But it suffered setbacks in Hungary, Holland, and England, where his doctrine was judged abominable, and where it was refused admission. However, the troubles which arose in England, under Charles I and Cromwell, gave occasion to the Deists, the Socinians, and all sorts of heretics, to preach their doctrine publicly. This was a resource for the Socinians, who had lost their favour in Poland, and who were very happy to be able to associate themselves with the Independents, who then formed a great party in England. The resemblance between the principles of the Quakers and the Socinians unites them in a particular manner, without the Episcopalians or the Presbyterians being able to prevent it. In 1690, during the descent of William of Nassau in England, the Socinians united again with the Non-Conformists to preserve their existence under the new government; for it is to be remarked that this society has never been tolerated in England, except by means of its associations; it has never been able to obtain public teaching, nor private worship, so revolting have her principles always been.

It is easy to understand why the Freemasons have never dared to recognise, in public, their true origin, or to profess their maxims in the eyes of society. If they had shown themselves undisguised for what they are, no Catholic state could have tolerated them in its bosom. That is why they wrap themselves in the veil of mysteries and symbols, and only make themselves known to men whom they have bound to their systems by horrible oaths, and whom they have tested for a long time before revealing anything essential to them.

To give themselves a religious air, they borrowed the symbols of a figurative religion, and have thus sought to obtrude on unthinking people. It is a question of revealing today their great secret, and of making them known for what they are. We will then see if there is no secret in Freemasonry, as many affect to declare; if it is not but a society of people who meet for amusement, or if this society is to become universal, and the model for all those which are authorised by the governments of Europe. I know that for a long time our philosophers have been busy giving Masonic societies all the perfection of which philosophy is capable. M. de Condorcet has drawn up a draft code, composed in part of the codes drawn up in 1779 by the assembly of Masons, which follow the system of Rectified Freemasonry.[2] M. Beguillet,[3] lawyer, composed six

---

2   The Rectified Scottish Rite resulted from the reforms of the Rite of Strict Observance by Jean-Baptiste Willermoz at the Congress of Lyon in 1778 and further transformation and evolution at the Congress of Willemsbad in 1782. Cf. John Robison, *Proofs of a Conspiracy* (London: Spradabach, 2022 [1797]). —Ed.

3   Edme Beguillet (d. 1786), also an agronomer and historian. —

discourses on high Masonry, to initiate Masons in the principles of high philosophy, lessons of which were given to the mysteries of Eleusis and Isis. The first speech turns to the works of the great Architect in the creation of the universe, and the second to the harmony of the spheres and the great chain of beings. It is a compendium of Plato's ideas on harmony and of those of the Gnostics, Valentinians, and early heretics who blended religious ideas with the principles of Eastern philosophy. The third discourse treats of Masonic history: in the last three he deals with the ranks, symbols, regulations, duties, and pleasures of Freemasons. Finally, the author of the *Essai sur la Franc-Maçonnerie* has given the plan on which all the lodges could be organised, which he believes capable of uniting all the sects of Freemasons, and of putting an end to the division of the lodges; but as it presupposes the study of the higher sciences, and the practice of the most exact duties of civil life, it can only be suitable for a small number Freemasons, that is to say, for philosophers and well-educated, worldly people; but all these plans, far from contradicting the origin we give to Freemasonry, they, on the contrary, only confirm it, as we will prove in the following.

Ed.

CHAPTER II

Masonic Lodges and Their Regime

fter having explained the origin of the f.-m., and defined what a Freemason is, it is appropriate to give an idea of the regime of this society, not quite according to bastard or badly organised lodges, but according to the ideas of the greatest masters, and the plan of Rectified Masonry.

The name of lodge is given both to the assembly of Freemasons and to the place where they are assembled. They have no fixed abode, because every Freemason regards himself as cosmopolitan, and because Masonry being a spiritual work, in the judgment of its teachers, it does not absolutely require a place to be formed.

'The reach of a lodge,' says the author of the *Essai sur la franc-maçonnerie,* 'extends from East to West. Its breadth is from North to South; its height is cubits without number.'

It follows that the whole universe forms but one lodge, that all the lodges are sisters, and all who gather therein, brothers; that they must all tend to the same goal. But as they cannot all be equally instructed, there must necessarily be school lodges and instructress lodges; ruling lodges and directed lodges; and therefore brothers who instruct and brothers who listen. Such is the graduated scale of Masonic lodges.

They usually choose as lodge a place where there are three ground floor chambers, at different orientations; one facing East, the other to the South, and the third to the North. But for greater convenience, when the premises permit, whenever possible they seek seven rooms: 1°. an antechamber; 2°. a preparation room; 3°. two dressing rooms; 4°. a storage unit; 5°. an archive room; 6°. an apartment for the lodge keeper.

In the antechamber, is a cabinet to keep the jewels, the clothes, and all the small utensils of the lodge. The preparation room is very small: the lodge rooms are proportionate to the number of Mason brothers; that of apprentices and fellowcrafts is greater than that of masters; but, as far as possible, they are one-third longer than their width; so, a lodge eighteen feet wide, must be twenty-four in length. The entrance door to each of these rooms faces the place of the Worshipful Master. The archive room contains the boxes and lodge papers, its constitutive letters patent, the state of its furniture, the rituals and the registers of the various grades, and the necessary books. In the storage room are kept large pieces of furniture.

There are in the lodge three dignitaries, to wit: a chief with the title of the *vénérable*, and two wardens; there are three officers, the orator, the librarian, and the treasurer. There are three degrees, the almoner, the master of ceremonies and the bursar. The lodge is inspected by a Grand Master or by one of his representatives.

Not only is the lodge composed of these officers, it is also composed of Apprentices, Fellowcrafts, Masters; Perfect Masters or Scotmen, and Perfect Architects or Scotmen that we also called Knight Masons. The Apprentice Mason is the brother who has been initiated into the first mysteries of Freemasonry, to study its purpose, secrets, and mysteries. The Fellowcraft is he who, being sufficiently instructed in the mysteries of Freemasonry, the doctrine of which was developed for him in the Masonic apprenticeship, is admitted and initiated into the next degree, called Fellow Craft. Master Masons are those who; having passed through the first two degrees, are received into the order of Freemasonry, to work under the direction of the architects, whose name indicates that they are the principal Masonic workmen. The Perfect Master possesses the art of Masonic work, has superintendence of it, and enjoys the honour attached to it.

Notwithstanding the liberty and equality that Masons profess in their lodges, they have servant brethren who are external guardians of the temples of Masonry. This word temple was given to Masonic lodges in imitation of the Templars who call their houses temples. This denomination seems all the better to suit the Freemasons, as they regard themselves as the successors of the order of the Templars.

Lodges are held for each degree in particular, and successively; 1°. when there is some instruction to be given, and it is indicated under the name of lodge of instruction, either for the mechanism of the degrees or to explain the spirit of them; 2°. when it is necessary to celebrate some feasts of the order, or at the four great feasts of the year; 3°. when there is any reception, or some extraordinary affair; 4°. in all cases where it is a question of making a few donations to traveling brothers, to the poor relatives of some brothers, or to receive visits from some dignitaries of the order.

Several payments are made every year in the lodge. The first is called capitation, and relates to the annual tax paid by the Masons of each lodge, to meet the expenses of the lodge, the hiring of the apartments, and the expenses incurred for wood, light, paper, wax, letters, etc. The second payment is called *écu d'ordre*, and consists of a sum of six livres, which all masons are obliged to pay each year at St John's Day. The third concerns the right of Masonic patents for the objects received from the directory general, which is in charge of the printing of all that concerns Masonry and they do not want known to the profane. The fourth payment is called an endowment, and is paid upon reception of each degree, and before it is granted. There are, besides, the pecuniary fines paid when there is a breach of police ordinances, the liberalities intended for institutions and collections for the poor, wayfarers, and the good works recommended to the generosity of the brothers.

According to the new organisation of Rectified Masonry, and according to the Masonic Code and the *Essai sur la franc-maçonnerie*, Europe has been divided into nine main parts. The number nine is a mysterious number for a Freemason, because it is the square of the number three, or of the three letters which compose in Hebrew the word *Jehovah*, which is, according to the Freemasons, the name of the great Architect of the universe, and the summary of the attributes of the Divinity, divided, according to the rabbis or the Kabbalah, in eighty-one attributes in the name of the Divinity, extracted from the Holy Scriptures. They make on this plan a magic square, where the number nine is marvellously distributed. Multiplied by three, it gives twenty-seven; this number multiplied by three gives eighty-one, which is the perfect number by which the number of lights which light up the reception of a Scottish Master is regulated.

The nine Masonic parts, in which Europe is divided, are called departments or districts; each large district is divided into nine cantons; each canton forms the territory of a Scottish Grand Lodge. The district in which the different lodges are situated, which it is deemed expedient to establish there, form a prefecture. The principal lodge of a prefecture is called a chapter or prefectural college. The prefectural chapter appoints a certain number of architects to direct the work of the lodges in the places where they are domiciled. Knight Masons of a lodge, when dealing with matters that pertain squarely to their degree, are said to be assembled in a commandery.

The functions of the Knight Masons, thus united, consist in supervising the instruction of the Freemasons of the first four degrees; to enforce the laws or statutes of Freemasonry; to judge, in the first instance, the disagreements which arise in the lodges of the district of the commandery; to regulate the destination of the benevolent donations coming from the fund for the poor and of the capitation surplus and the donations from the brothers, who will have intended the sum given to be employed in the district of the commandery; finally, to direct the benevolent institutions which the prefectural college shall have established in the arrondissement of the commandery, and to direct them in conformity with the decrees of the prefectural college.

The Commander is the leader of all the Knights Masons of his district; he is the superior of the students of Freemasonry.

The oldest knight of a district is the senior of the commandery; he supervises the administration, takes care of its good order, and is adviser to the commander.

The chapter, or the prefectural college, is the assembly of all the Knight Masons of a prefecture, present individually or represented by their commanders. It forms the court of lodges; this chapter is made up of nine knight masons, heads of nine commanderies in the district. They have, in the chapter, capitular charges, to wit: prefect, banneret, senior, chancellor, scholar, treasurer, hospitaller, secretary, vice-chancellor, and master of ceremonies. The prefect is president of the chapter, and the man of the order of the knights; the banneret represented the nobility; the senior was the deputy of the clergy; but these two abolished bodies will no longer have representatives. The chancellor is the depositary of seals, registers, and the custodian of records and titles. It is to him that they send everything addressed to the chapter; it is by him or by his secretaries that everything is written and sealed.

Since each department has its general assembly, if the prefectural chapter is made up of nine commanders, the priory chapter is composed of nine prefects, where a president is the prefect. The provincial chapter is composed of nine priors, including a president, the provincial grand master. Finally, the general chapter is made up of nine provincial grand masters, including a president, the grand-master general.

The first tribunal of a lodge is called a committee; the second is called the college of Masonic Knights, it is permanent; the third is accidental, and is called a tribunal of conciliation. The committee of the lodge is composed of the venerable, the first and second wardens, the orator, the keeper of the seals, and the treasurer. It is this committee that prepares the matters to be dealt with by the lodge; that settles the ordinary expenses of the lodge; that judges matters of slight importance.

The college of knights judges the lodge's important matters, which are not within the competence of the committee; and, by summons, all those who are of its competence.

The conciliation committee is intended to settle contentious disputes among the brothers, in order to prevent them from having recourse to the means, often ruinous, of justice.

The priory directory is the common centre of communications of the different sites and like the soul of the machine. Through it all information circulates, the union is maintained and the fraternal bond is consolidated. The general management board maintains correspondence with the other management boards; he writes the registry of deliberations.

The great directory issues the codes, rituals, tables, patents of each newly established lodge.

The prefect, the chancellor, and the commander of the lodge perform the installation ceremony; the first by virtue of his dignity; the second for the inspection of the site; the third as immediate superior and representative of the lodge of the general chapter.

The fundamental principles of Masonry are liberty and equality; these are also the principles of republican laws. The Masonic constitution is therefore of the nature of the republics. In these, the people as a body have the sovereign power, and form a democratic government. Freemasons have the right to create laws for themselves; the sovereign power therefore resides in the Masonic body, and its government is therefore also democratic.

Republics have always been divided into classes or cantons, and it is on this division has depended the duration of their existence. The United Provinces of America[1] are divided into states; the states, like Carolina, into counties, districts, and parishes. Holland is divided into provinces; the Swiss are in cantons; the Roman republic was divided into tributes, and was afterwards divided into provinces. The Freemasons therefore had to divide them-

---

1 A name used by the French to designate the thirteen British colonies. Just prior to declaring independence, what later became the United States used the term United Colonies to refer to the aforementioned thirteen as a whole. It was used at the Second Continental Congress and was use colloquially between 1775 and 1776. —Ed.

selves almost in the same way, as much as their present state of dependence must have prescribed to them; and it is on this plan that the organization of the Masonic order is made, after having passed through many trials, the variations necessitated by the unfortunate circumstances in which they have found themselves. There are still today only a small number of lodges which have consented to accept this regime made to subdue the entire universe; the others, which may be regarded as bastard lodges, cling to an ancient regime which they will abandon in the measure that men relish the prize of liberty and equality.

CHAPTER III

What the National Assembly Owes to Freemasonry

t is difficult to explain how much the National Assembly of France owes to Freemasonry. Many Frenchmen are still convinced today it was national despotism, the stubbornness of the nobility and the clergy that forced the assembly to form itself into a national assembly, and to attack pitilessly all the abuses that reigned under the ancient regime. These Frenchmen, who are ignorant of the influence of the Masonic government, not only in the lodges of Rectified Masonry, but in the clubs spread over the whole territory of France, in the departments and districts, in the committees and the very National Assembly, are every day duped by their affability, the appearances, and the speeches they print, are displayed, and a thousand bribed mouths proclaim everywhere. However, the truth is that before the States-General were convoked, all Freemasons spoke only of raising their Grand Master to some important post as long as they were able to appear in the first rank, and he give them great consideration. They spared nothing to achieve their purpose. The splendours of the French empire will transmit to posterity the incredible efforts the Freemasons have made, in all the provinces, to engage all the French to unite with them to abolish everything that could remind of the ancient regime, and replace it with what pertained to their association, which was designed, according to them, to remind all men of freedom and the primitive equality for which man was born.

The National Assembly has favoured with all its power the projects of the Masonic order; we can judge it by the adoption which it made of the latter's government, its maxims, and by the passion with which it gave support to everything suggested by the society of Masons through its clubs, its associations, and its writings.

It should be noted first that the National Assembly, while saying that it wanted a monarchical government, that the king had never been more king than he would be through his decrees, nevertheless ended up adopting a republican government and a pure democracy; and it borrowed its organisation from Freemasonry. To be convinced of this, let us

examine the division which it made of the kingdom; it is absolutely the same as that of Masonry,
not only as to mode, but as to the name itself.

The government of Freemasonry is divided into
departments, districts, cantons, arrondissements;
what the National Assembly has decreed is distributed according to the same divisions. The municipalities answer to the lodges, which, corresponding
to a common centre, form a canton. A determined
number of cantons, corresponding to a new centre, form a district; several arrondissements have
formed a district, and several districts have composed a department; the departments have a common centre in the National Assembly where all
the citizens of the kingdom concur, through their
representatives, in making decisions, laws, and to
form a great republic.

In Freemasonry, the general directory com-
municates with the particular directories, and
through them the whole machine is set in motion.
The directory of the National Assembly, which cor-
responds with the directories of the departments,
produces the same effect.

All the lodges of a district, in the Masonic government, are equal among themselves; all the
municipalities are also so according to the organisation they have received from the National
Assembly. The first court of a Masonic lodge is
called committee, and its purpose is to prepare the
matters which are to be treated in the lodge, and
to judge matters of slight importance; it is in the

same spirit and for the same end that the National Assembly has formed committees, has permitted the districts to form themselves into committees to prepare the matters on which it would report.

The justices of the peace act as the committee of conciliation, and have the same attribution. All Freemasons are judges in the lodge; all the French are also so in their territory, which is a grand lodge. It is in their presence that the cause of the accused is pleaded, and their judgment is what makes the law. Such was the judgment of M. de Favras,[1] such is what the people passed in all the places where they assembled, and on all the matters which they judged within their competence.

The duties of the terrible brother, the grand inquisitor of the Masonic lodges, are performed among us by the Search Committee, which is presided over by the terrible brother Voidel.[2]

---

1   A Royalist, Thomas de Mahy, Marquis de Favras (26 March 1744 – 18 February 1790) ended up being arrested, accused of being involved in a plot to free Louis XVI from the Tuilleries; spirit him, Marie Antoinette, and their chidren out of the country; and install the Count de Provence as regent with absolute power, something deemed by the revolutionary authorities a crime against the nation. At the trial his accusers failed to produce sufficient evidence, however, but an attempt to free him by a group of Royalists led to his being sentenced to hanging. At his execution, he is reputed to have said, upon reading the warrant, 'I see that you have made three spelling mistakes'. Subsequently, his wife was granted a pension by the King and under the restoration his son was given an allowance by Louis XVIII.—Ed.

2   In 1790 Jean-Georges-Charles Voidel (1758 - 1812) had become a member of this committee (comité des recherches),

The syndic attorneys, the district attorneys, the commune attorneys of each municipality, perform the functions of the orator of each lodge; it is they who watch over the observance of laws and statutes, who press for their execution, who lodge complaints against refractory parties, who take it upon themselves to speak in all matters of consequence, who are, in a word, the organ of the public voice.

The order which Masonry has established among its degrees, in its lodges, and in its tribunals, is the same as the assembly has adopted among the officers to whom it has entrusted a portion of its authority. The National Guards are subordinate to municipal authority as Apprentices, Fellow Craft, and Master Masons are to the authority of the dignitaries and officers of a lodge. The operations of the district are submitted to its court, or to the department to which it belongs when it is formed into a directory. Everywhere there reigns a subordination and a reaction, which should maintain peace and good order everywhere if all Frenchmen and all Masons stifle the voice of passions, so as to listen only to that of justice and truth.

The sashes with which the National Assembly has decorated municipal officers are also borrowed

---

which served as the police, along with Poulain de Corbion, Abbé Joubert, de Pardieu, Ledéan, Cochon de l'Apparent, Payen-Boisneuf, Verchère de Reffye, Rousselet, de Macaye, de Genlis, and Babey. He subsequently came to head this committee, in which capacity he became a powerful figure. —Ed.

from Freemasonry. It is the first ornament with which they honour an apprentice Mason: after its receipt, they gird him with a sash with a serrated tassel, which perfectly resembles the civic sash. The hat granted for distinction to our judges is still borrowed from Masonry. The plume with which it is adorned makes it somewhat resemble the hat of the venerable and the feathered toque of the overseers; I don't know if even the custom that has been introduced for some time of tying shoes with silk ribbons did not originate from Freemasonry.

How much resemblance indeed do we not notice between the Masonic assemblies, and the august National Assembly of the French? The society of Masons has an outer doctrine and an inner one; a doctrine known to the first chiefs of the inner administration of the lodges, and a doctrine which is limited to the mechanism of degrees; a doctrine which is known only to the first officers of the high ranks, which are like the soul of the whole society; a doctrine with which they amuse young apprentices, which is susceptible of all sorts of favourable interpretations.

Doesn't the National Assembly also have a double doctrine, one which is known only to what are called the makers, and another which is public, the meaning of which each imagines himself to grasp? A doctrine of which the committees and some members on the Left have the key; and another doctrine which is made for those whose suffrage is necessary, but whom they do not seek to give in-depth knowledge of the designs of the assembly? How many are there whose opinions are fixed by the single cry of aristocrat and democrat? It is a war cry which calls to arms, like in the past the cry of Montjoye, Saint-Denis, and which they have mean anything they want.

The very system of the Assembly is completely Masonic, it is the same manner of soliciting speech, permission; to deliberate, to lodge a complaint, to maintain order. The bell has the same effect as the gavel; they ring to order as the drum brother strkes to order. I am not surprised that the French have easily become accustomed to this scheme; most of them are Freemasons, so they found themselves fully trained in this little exercise; and those who were not acquainted with it, have marvelled at the ease with which the National Assembly has become familiar with the regime it has made for itself.

The oath that the National Assembly demanded of the French has the same origin, and has produced enthusiasm among the Masons, who have been delighted to see their citizens binding themselves together and tightening the knots to their fatherland, as they themselves pledged allegiance to Masonic society through a dreadful oath, without knowing the nature of the commitments they were about to contract. The more it encountered refractories who disdained or rejected the oath required of them, the more they appeared odious to the Freemasons, who censured their conduct and who banded together to prosecute them with the blind relentlessness of sectarians who want to proselytise at whatever price.

And to feel how much the Masonic regime is dear to the National Assembly, it suffices to remember that it abolished all corporations, except the Freemasons'; the former even seconds, as far as the latter is in it, the maxims of this society, supporting them with all its authority. When one enters the lodge, every Freemason or foreigner must deposit, in the antechamber or the vestibule of the lodge, all that characterises his nobility, his birth, his titles, the grades; everything must yield to the cords and jewels of order; there are only those which are sacred, which do not offend self-esteem, which excite neither murmurs nor envy. By an equal principle, or rather by the same, the National Assembly has proscribed blue cords, the ornaments of all the orders, the orders themselves, to leave only the Masonic ribbons, only the jewels of the order, only the ranks and the distinctions which are received there. It has not yet pronounced that there are only those with whom one can adorn oneself in the eyes of society; but it reserves the right to give its decision on this point, when its projects have acquired the maturity that time and patience nurture for them.

Even the commissioners, whom the assembly detaches from its bosom, remind us of the image of Freemasonry; they hold the rank of Masonic visitors and inspectors; and the Assembly bestowed upon them the same honours, because they have been chosen from the number of those who are, in its eyes, the most respectable.

I forgot to say that in the form of the elections, the choice of voters, the qualities that are required in them, the advice given to them, the Assembly seems to have imitated everything from Free-masonry. The conduct prescribed for municipal officers, for the members of the departments, is absolutely modelled on what is recommended to the venerable, who presides over a lodge; that is to say, gentleness, prudence, discretion, a lot of skill to handle minds, a patience that is discouraged by nothing, courage, and magnanimity.

The patent rights established in Freemasonry have also been adopted by the National Assembly, which will owe all their inventions to this society. Wasn't it convenient that all those who are invited to defend the Masonic constitution should, like the Freemasons, be adorned with cockades and armed with swords, sabres, etc.? That was the object of the great armament of the National Guard.

They were well assured of pleasing the National Assembly when they made it pass under the arch of steel, the greatest honour which Freemasons render to those they respect, when it was in a body at the *Te Deum* sung at the Cathedral of Paris at the beginning of the Revolution. This ceremony proves both the number of Freemasons who are in the National Guard, and the number of those who are in the Assembly, who felt the value of the hon-our rendered to them. I judge it by what a Freemason said to me one day, that the signs by which they recognize each other made an impression on them for which he could not fully account, but which had a marvellous effect.

The military officers, almost all of whom were nobles, the magistrates of all ranks who had been received as Freemasons before the revolution, should not have been surprised when they saw the execution on a grand scale of what they had professed in small; but the ecclesiastics, who are more ignorant of what passes in the lodge, and who serve God according to the principles of re-vealed religion taught by the Catholic Church, are much more foreign to this new inauguration, and less suited to adopt the plan. Their repugnance will be still more pronounced when they have read the following chapters.

CHAPTER IV

The Society of Freemasons Has Changed France's Morals

urope is amazed at the change that has taken place in our morals. In the past, a Frenchman was only re-proached for his gaiety, his levity, his frivolity: today, when he has become cruel, barbarous, bloodthirsty, we abhor him, and we fear him as one would a ferocious beast. Who has made him fierce, suspicious, always ready to make an attempt on the lives of fellow men, and to feast on the picture of death? Shall I say it, and will you believe me? It is Freemasonry, not that which claims to be rectified, and which claims to be governed only by reason; but this Freemasonry which provided the heroes of the French revolution. Yes,

I am not afraid to put it forward, it is Freemasonry which taught the French to consider death in cold blood, to wield the dagger with fearlessness, to eat the flesh of the dead, to drink from their skulls, and to surpass the savage peoples in barbarism and cruelty.

Under the prestige of liberty and equality, it has known how to extinguish the sentiment of Religion in the hearts of the French; to render odious to them their princes, their magistrates, their most faithful pastors; to nurture a spirit of division in the bosom of the most united families; to inspire horror and carnage to make it mad projects succeed. It is in the shadow of inviolable secrecy that it makes initiates swear to her mysteries, that it has given lessons in murder, in assassination, arson, and cruelties. It encouraged the most unheard-of crimes, by the assurance of impunity, by the number of arms armed for the defence of those who would follow its maxims; and it succeeded in taking away the severity of the law, whatever excesses they permitted themselves. Of what, indeed, is not capable an ambitious society, guided by fanaticism; which has connections all over Europe; which has linked to his cause an infinity of individuals who have sworn to come to its aid, whatever the cost to them; which seems made to unite the heretics of all sects, and which sees them already prepared to move at the first signal?

Although the degrees of elect masons are only preparations for the great Masonic initiation, yet, in play-acting our mysteries, that is to say, the birth of *Jesus Christ* and the Persecution of Herod, the adoration of the Magi and their return to their country, finally the death and passion of *Jesus Christ*, the Freemasons have found the secret to inspire initiates to their mysteries, the greatest nerve, and the greatest intrepidity.

In the reception of the first degree of elect, all the brothers are dressed in black, and wear a small breastplate on the left side, on which is embroidered a skull, with a bone and a silver dagger in saltire; all surrounded by the motto: *Vaincre ou mourir*. They have a large, lustrous black cord, four fingers wide, hanging from right to left, bearing on the front: *Vaincre ou mourir*. At the bottom of the cord is a white ribbon rosette, at the end of which hangs a dagger in its sheath. The apron is of white leather, bordered in black; on the bib is embroidered a skull with a bone and a sword in saltire, below a compass embroidered in gold. On the pocket of the apron is a large teardrop, at the bottom and on the sides eight other smaller teardrops; at the end of the pocket is an acacia branch.

All these signs of death become more frightening by the way in which the candidate is questioned. After giving him bloody gloves, blindfolding him, and putting a dagger to his heart, they pretend that he has been guilty of a great crime in carrying out what he has been ordered to do; but he finally gets his grace, when he assures that he delivered *Hiram Abif*, in killing the lion, the tiger, and the bear, which represent Herod, king of the Jews. The lion is the sign of his power, the tiger represents his cruelty, and the bear the barbarism with which he is reproached towards his children.

The oath required of the candidate is something horrible. Here it is: 'After my eyes have been deprived of the light by the hot iron, I consent, if I ever reveal the secret which will be entrusted to me, that my body become prey to the vultures; that my memory be in execration to the children of the widow throughout the earth, so be it'. This widow is the Socinian society.

What follows this oath is no less frightening; the candidate is placed in a dark room, draped in black: depicted on one side, is a cave covered with the branches of trees, and a ghost sitting on the branches. Its head is furnished with hair, but only resting on the body; below is a table with a seat, and opposite a transparent picture, an arm holding a dagger and a lamp, which it can take by hand: on the other side is a fountain, whose water flows drop by drop into a vase made of brass, to make the sound higher pitched.

At the given signal, the candidate placed in this apartment, sits down on the stool, and rests his head on his left hand, to consider more calmly what is under his eyes. The intimate brother says to him: 'Do not move, my brother, from this situation, until you hear three knocks, which will serve as a signal to uncover your eyes.' This sign is given, and time is allowed for the candidate to examine, by the light of a feeble lamp placed in this dark place, all the objects that surround him, and that are very likely to freeze him with terror. Then the intimate brother returns and makes him drink a glass of water, telling him that he still has a lot of work to do.

'Take,' he says, 'this lamp, arm yourself with this dagger, enter the depths of this cave, strike all you find who will resist you, defend yourself, avenge your master, and make yourself worthy of being elected.'

The candidate enters, dagger raised, holding the lamp in his left hand. The intimate brother follows him, and shouts, showing him the ghost: Strike, avenge Hiram, here is his assassin. The candidate strikes with his dagger, and blood flows in great streams; then the intimate brother said to him: 'Leave this lamp, take this head by the hair, raise your dagger and follow me.'

If we wanted to train assassins, would we go about it differently to accustom them to the horrors of death, and make them stifle the remorse of a conscience which would be susceptible of being alarmed? If this is not the school that taught the murderers of Foulon and Bertier, Belsunce[1] and so

---

1   Joseph Foulon de Doué, Intendant of Finance, had the honour, in 1789, of being the first to be hung by a lamp post; because the rope broke three times, his head was severed and then paraded with the mouth stuffed with grass, hay, and excrement. Said severed head was then presented to his son-in-law, Bertier de Sauvigny, Intendant of Paris, in whose home Foulon had sought refuge, and who was also hung from a lamppost,

many other unfortunate victims of fanatical fury, it will be admitted at least that before the society of the Socinians was established in France under the name of Freemasonry, the French had never, in the midst of the horrors of civil wars, been inclined by some ferocious instinct to atrocities like those of which all the provinces of the kingdom have furnished us with so many unfortunate examples.

It is not in a single degree that these lessons of savage cruelty are given; the reception of the fifteen elect, accustoms the candidates to carry, in their hands, the heads of those they have murdered. Having been received, they place them in an apartment draped in black, in the corners of which are placed three large skeletons, which are claimed to represent the corpses of Hiram's three assassins. They put two skulls in both hands of each candidate; that of the right hand has the jaw crossed by a dagger. It is through this exercise that the French have been accustomed to carry in their hands, or to raise at the end of a pike, the heads of those whom they had assassinated, and to feast all eyes on this spectacle of blood, as the barbarous peoples hung at their door, or in a public place, the heads of animals which they had killed in hunting. In several places, they drank the blood of those

---

accused of having been the cause of food shortages. Henri de Belsunce was shot in the head, cut open, had his entrails ripped out and thrown into a fire, wherefrom, taking the lead from a hungry woman who took the roasted heart to eat, the rest of mob helped themselves in a similar fashion. —Ed.

whom they had, in a blind fury, inhumanly immolated; they ate the heart and the flesh of French citizens; and it is Christians who have gone to such excesses of barbarism! No, it was only Freemasonry that learnt to eat human flesh, persuading its initiates that it gives them Hiram's brains to eat in its fanatical ceremonies.

There is no one who does not agree that there is an outrageous fanaticism, a barbarism without example, perhaps even among cannibals, which can lead men naturally gentle and humane to excesses which make hair stand on end in horror. Now, this fanaticism is found in Freemasonry and nowhere else.

When they announce the candidate among elect, to the mightiest Solomon, this candidate is barefoot and blindfolded; the introducing brother knocks nine times, which is answered by Brother Adoniram. He is allowed to enter and the venerable, who is then called the mightiest Solomon, asks him if he is in a condition to shed the last drop of his blood, to avenge the first drop of the respectable master Adoniram. The answer of the candidate is a very decided yes, although he does not yet know in whose name he thus undertakes to shed his blood. The sign he receives from the venerable is a stab on the forehead, accompanied by the word Vengeance.

If all this ceremony were only an amusement, you will admit to me that, for men of all conditions, it is an apprenticeship in cruelty; that this is the form of treason which we have not yet been able to define; since it tends to remove, from the fatherland and from France, a crowd of good citizens; since it perverts the national spirit, the genius and the hearts of France; since, if this practice becomes accepted, France will become a place of assassins and the scourge of nations.

The very oath of this degree exudes cruelty. Whoever pronounces it undertakes and agrees to have his body cut open, his head cut off, so that it may be presented to the Grand Master, if he reveals the place of his reception, those who attended, or the secret entrusted to him.

All these oaths are dreadful, criminal, and justly condemned by the Popes and Doctors of the Catholic Church, and should be so by all thinking persons. But the one pronounced in the sect of the Illuminati, which is a branch of Freemasonry, is even more revolting. Here it is as it is found in the Red Lodge and in the life of Cagliostro (Avertis, p. 9).

The candidate is led through a dark corridor, into an immense room, whose vault, parquet floor, and walls, are covered with a black cloth, strewn with red flames and threatening snakes; three sepulchral lamps throw from time to time a dying light, and barely allow us to distinguish, in this lugubrious enclosure, the remains of death, supported by funereal crapes. Part of a skeleton forms, in the middle, a sort of altar; next to it stand books; some contain threats against perjury; the others, the funest history of the revenges of the invisible spirit, and of the infernal evocations they utter for a long time in vain.

Eight hours pass. Then ghosts, dragging mortuary veils, slowly cross the hall, and sink into underground passages, without the sound of trapdoors being heard, nor that of their drop. You only notice the foul smell they exhale.

The initiate remains twenty-four hours in this dark asylum, in the midst of a chilling silence. A severe fast had already weakened his thoughts: prepared liqueurs began by tiring, and ended by exhausting his senses. At his feet are placed three cups of a greenish drink; need brings them closer to the lips, involuntary fear repels them.

Finally, two men appear who are taken for ministers of death. They encircle the forehead of the candidate with an aurora ribbon, dyed with blood and inscribed with silver characters, intermingled with the figure of Our Lady of Loreto. They hang from his neck a kind of amulet, wrapped in a purple cloth; he receives a copper crucifix two inches long; he is stripped of his clothes, which two serving brothers place on a raised pyre at the other end of the hall. On his naked body they draw crosses in blood. In this state of suffering and humiliation, he sees approaching him, with great strides, five ghosts armed with a sword, covered in sheets dripping with blood. Their faces are veiled: they spread a carpet on the floor, kneel on it, pray to God, and remain on their chests, with their arms stretched and their faces against the ground, in profound silence. An hour passes in this painful posture. After this tiring ordeal, sorrowful accents are heard; the pyre is kindled, but casts only a pale glow; the clothes are consumed there. A colossal and even transparent figure emerges from the very heart of the pyre. At his sight, the five men prostrate, enter into convulsions unbearable to see: images too faithful of these foaming struggles, where a mortal, taken with a sudden illness, ends up being overwhelmed by it.

So a trembling voice pierces the vault, and utters the formula of the execrable oaths that must be pronounced. . . . My pen hesitates, and I feel almost guilty relating them.

'In the name of Jesus crucified, swear to break the carnal ties that still bind you to father, to mother, brothers, sisters, husbands, relatives, friends, mistresses, laws, chiefs, benefactors, and any being whatsoever to whom you have promised faith, obedience, gratitude or service.

'Name the place where you were born, in order to exist in another sphere, where you will not arrive until you have abjured this pestilent globe, vile scum of the heavens.

'From this moment you are freed from the so-called oath made to this country and its laws. Swear to reveal to the new chief you recognise, whatever you have seen or done, taken, read, or heard, learned or guessed, and even to seek, to spy on whatever is not offered to your eyes.

'Honour and respect aqua Toffana, as a prompt, sure, and necessary means of purging the globe through death or dulling of the faculties of those who seek to debase the truth, or to tear it from our hands.

'Flee Spain, flee Naples, flee all accursed lands; flee, finally, the temptation to reveal what you hear: because thunder is no quicker than the knife that will reach you wherever you may be.'

When the patient has pronounced these words, a candelabrum is placed before him, with seven black candles; at his feet a vase full of human blood in which his body is washed. He drinks half a glass of it, and he utters the fatal oath. A cold sweat arises from his livid cheeks; he can barely stand on his failing legs. The brothers bow down; and he, trembling, torn with remorse, thrown into a species of delirium awaits his destiny. Immediately after the ceremony, they throw him into a bath, and serve him a meal of root vegetables.

Perhaps, it will be said, Freemasonry has not adopted all these excesses? I answer that there is none of which it is not capable, and which one cannot justly impute to it according to its constitutional principles. It wants and pretends to bring all sects into her bosom; therefore those which are moderate will be found next to those which are fierce, extreme in their principles. Thus, by its own admission, it will find itself formed of contradictory sects that will have opposing principles, that will be capable of approving and teaching what others will find reprehensible and untenable: therefore the principles of the Freemasons tend to form a monstrous body, capable of all the excesses in which error and fanaticism can lead a man who is weak and blinded by prejudices and false opinions: isn't there, in the Masonic lodges, a mixture of Lutherans and Protestants, of Christians and Deists, of Jews and Mahometans, who can all be received in a lodge? Wouldn't that be enough to deter a good Catholic from being received there?

Do not the Apostles St. John and St Paul teach, in their Epistle to all the faithful, to flee the society of heretics, if one does not want to expose one's faith to the danger of foundering?

CHAPTER V

Freemasonry Aims to Destroy the Christian Religion

uch an imputation requires proof, and proofs that Freemasons cannot disavow; I will therefore draw them from the instructions which are given to all Freemasons, and which are like the first elements of Freemasonry.

Every Christian knows and firmly believes that the entire Christian Religion is founded on *Jesus Christ*: that He is not only its foundation, but also its perfection and end. Remove *Jesus Christ*: to Christians, it is to deprive them of their whole religion, with all the succours of the present life, and all the consolations of the future life: now, this is the principal and unique object of Freemasonry; it is to this point that all degrees return, all the emblems, all the hieroglyphs of this order.

It would have been too revolting to announce such an impious goal; and certainly the Freemasons could not have gained proselytes in the middle of this century, however corrupt it may have been, if they had announced their project in the open. What did they do to succeed? They cobbled together the reveries of the Kabbalah with historical features, and have made a mixture which resembles nothing else.

The bottleneck, and yet the capital point, was to deprive *Jesus Christ* of His divinity, His mission, and the power to work miracles by His own virtue. It was also necessary to make people hear, because they would not have dared to say it, that He was not risen, that He had not ascended to Heaven, that He had not founded the Christian Church, or at least that He was not the only one founder. They thought they could get through all this by inventing an absurd story on which all Freemasonry is based, and which is told seriously as a real event to those who are initiated in this society. Here it is, pretty much, let it be told.

> Adoniram was chosen by Solomon to have stewardship over the workers of the temple that he wanted to erect to the great Architect of the Universe. This steward, having a large number of workers to pay, in order to know them all, and to give to each the salary due to him according to his quality of apprentice, fellowcraft,

or master, agreed, with each of them, on different words, signs, and grips to distinguish them. Three fellowcrafts resolved to obtain the pay of master, using the words, signs, and grips peculiar to that grade. To this effect, they resolved to force Adoniram to reveal to them what distinguished the masters from the fellowcrafts, or to assassinate him. It was at the foot of the two brazen columns in the vestibule of the temple, one of which was called *Jachin* and the other *Boaz*, Hebrew names signifying strength and stability, where Adoniram was in the habit of rendering payment to his workmen. The three fellowcrafts, who wished to have the master's pay, hid themselves in the temple; they posted themselves one in the South, the other in the North, and the other in the East. When Adoniram, who entered the temple by the Western door, passed in front of that on the South, one of the three fellowcrafts asked him for the master's word, raising a stick above him. Adoniram told him that he had not received the master's word in this way. Immediately this fellowcraft struck him on the head with the stick. This blow not having been violent enough to throw Adoniram to the ground, he fled towards the Northern door, where he found the second fellowcraft, who treated him as had done the first. However, not having yet been struck down by this second blow, he was ready to leave by the Eastern door, but there he found the third fellowcraft who, after having made the same request to him as the first two, assassinated him without mercy: after which the three assassins joined to bury him. Once inhumed, they cut a branch from an acacia tree nearby, and laid it in the place where the corpse had been deposited, to recognise it when visible to them.

Solomon having spent seven days without seeing Adoniram, ordered the seventh master to look for him; and for this purpose, first to go and place themselves three at each door of the temple to find out what had become of him. These nine masters punctually executed the order given to them; and after having searched for a long time, without acquiring any news about Adoniram, three of them, who found themselves a little tired, went to rest near the place where he was buried. One of the three, to sit down more easily, put his hand to the branch of acacia, which immediately gave way. Then his companions noticed that the earth in this place had been newly disturbed. Wanting to know the cause, they began to search until they found the body of Adoniram. Surprised and astonished at this discovery, they made a sign to the other masters to come to them, and all easily recognised Adoniram, whom they suspected of had been assassinated by some fellowcrafts who had wanted him to reveal to them the master's word. Fearing that they would have taken it from him, they agreed on another, which would be the word that one of them would pronounce when removing the corpse. There was one who took him by a finger, and this finger remained in his hand; he took it immediately by another finger, which remained the same; he then seized him by the wrist, which was detached from the arm, which made him pronounce *macbenac*, the flesh leaving the bones. All the masters then agreed that that would be the master's word. After having exhumed the corpse, they made their

report to Solomon who, to show the esteem he
had for Adoniram, ordered that he be buried in
his temple with great ceremony.

There is no one who does not feel that this story
is implausible, and that it has all the appearance
of a tale invented at pleasure. However, it on the
basis of this story that was founded the Masonry
called, for this reason, *Adoniramite.* In the higher degrees, this Adoniram takes the name of *Hi-
ram-Abif,* which is interpreted as Hiram, high
priest, from which one can conclude that he is a
borrowed character, whom they have mean whatever they wish. But it is to be remarked that however implausible this story may be, it is not permissi-
ble for a Freemason to call it into doubt. However,
they are allowed to frighten young apprentices of
Adoniram's shadow, and to subject them to ridiculous and pleasant pranks for the amusement of
the masters.

But under this forced travesty, we can notice 1°.
acacia; 2°. the master's word; 3°. the three strokes
with the scroll or stick; 4°. the exhumation of the
corpse of Adoniram with the circumstances that
accompany it.

The acacia, according to the Freemasons, signifies the cross of *Jesus Christ*; the three strokes of
the roller or stick therefore signify the three nails
with which he was attached to the cross. The master's word that Adoniram did not want to communicate, is the great word of Jehovah: now, here is

the story of Adoniram brought closer to the truth.

It is certain, according to holy history, that Solomon appointed Adoniram to watch over the workmen occupied in the construction of the temple of Jerusalem; but what the Freemasons add in excess is drawn from the Chaldaic paraphrase, and borrowed from the tale that the rabbis weaved to deprive *Jesus Christ* of his divinity and power. They imagined that one day, having entered the temple of Jerusalem, he had seen the Holy of Holies, where the high priest alone had permission to enter; that he had secretly broken into, had found the word *Jehovah* there, which he had taken away, by putting it in an incision which he had made in his thigh, and that it was by virtue of this ineffable name that he had worked the miracles attributed to him.

However ridiculous this invention of the rabbis may be, the Socinians and the Freemasons have adopted it because it helps them to prove that *Jesus Christ* is not God, that he was only an attendant over the workmen of the great Architect of the Universe, of whom Solomon himself was but the minister. The circumstances which are supposed to have accompanied the discovery of the body of Adoniram are also intended to prove that *Jesus Christ* is not risen, since seven days after being buried, it was found that the flesh had left the bones; consequently, that he had fallen into corruption. If *Jesus Christ* is not risen, says the Apostle, our faith is vain; therefore, the whole system of revealed Religion is baseless.

This is the crucial point that Socinus and the Freemasons sought to establish. They did not try to make it fashionable by principle and discussion; they would not have succeeded; but they have invented a practical system that leads Christians to the abjuration of the Religion of *Jesus Christ*; and they have the skill to impose silence on all religious discussions, which could have brought to light what they with the greatest care wanted to hide, and to penalise all those who dared to transgress the regulations they have made on the subject. Such is the progress of Freemasonry, such is the great sect which the profane have not been able to penetrate up to this day, and which will be brought to light by the analysis of the degrees of Masonry, as soon as we choose to examine them.

The degree of the Rosicrucian reverses all belief in the real presence of *Jesus Christ* in the Holy Sacrament on our Altars. The supper is celebrated there in the manner of the Protestants, and with ceremonies which accompany the supper of the Jews; so that they profess there, by their actions, that everything happens figuratively in the Eucharist of Christians, and that they have as much respect, if not more, for the Masonic Supper as for the communion of the body and blood of *Jesus Christ*, in the Roman Catholic and Apostolic Church.

So let's not be surprised that Protestants unite with Freemasons to persecute the Catholic Religion. There are, on both sides, the same maxims, the same hatred. It is shown in the trial of Cagliostro, the founder of Egyptian Masonry, that he manifested in all places his hatred, and the most decided contempt for the whole system of the Catholic Religion, for its ministers, and for its practices. He attacked the majesty and the perfections of God, the divinity of *Jesus Christ*, His death, the great work of the redemption of the human race, the virginity of the Blessed Virgin, the efficacy of His Sacraments, the adoration of Saints, the dignity of the ecclesiastical hierarchy.

It is shown in all that has happened in France, on the part of the Protestants, that they have sworn the ruin of the Christian Religion. Those of Montauban have planned to drive out of the city all the unfortunate Catholics, those of Nismes have waged a cruel war against priests and Catholics. The secret committee of the Jacobin Club is almost entirely composed of Protestants, and it is in this club that the motions most opposed to Catholic principles are made.

The Freemasons have done their utmost before the National Assembly to overthrow from top to bottom the dogma and the morals of the Catholic Religion; and they partially succeeded. The French constitution is the summary of the clubs, where the Freemasons dominate; it was led by the Marquis de Condorcet and his adherents, and he is the Grand Doctor of Freemasonry; the Duke of Gold . . . . Grand Master of all the lodges of France, he has exhausted his fortune to establish this great work. A crowd of writers, enemies of the Christian religion, have lent their pens, and vomited blasphemies against what is holiest in it; municipal officers broke into the sacred tabernacles, took out the ciboriums, still full of hosts, with profane hands, and piled up, in their carriage and under their feet, ciboriums, chalices, monstrances, pronouncing impious blasphemies. What are all these men of iniquity? Deists, philosophers, Freemasons who want to unite everything under the flag of freedom of religion and freedom of government.

They do not say openly that they do not want to submit to religious mysteries other than theirs, that they reject the faith in *Jesus Christ*, and that they want to abolish His Religion; but they remove the instruments of His worship; they close the churches where the people used to assemble to pray to their God and Saviour; they pursue His ministers; they use force of the state, which is in their hands, to cause them to desert His temples; is this not to act as if they had abjured their religion, as if they wished to efface it from all hearts? The members of the National Assembly see all these insults and these profanations, and they do not prevent them: it seems that the National Assembly retains its activity only to protect the Protestants and their ministers; so it also wants to overthrow the Christian Religion? It suffices, to be convinced of this, to follow step by step the procedures of the members of this Assembly, and of those whom it has set in motion.

They had the skill to divide the Catholic clergy, in order to destroy it more easily. The pastors of the second order, whom the assembly had used to weaken the authority of the first pastors, were driven from their places, as the others had been from their seats. A fatal oath has disturbed all consciences, it has shaken all those whose faith was weak and made them fall: the churches have lost their legitimate pastors, who have been replaced by intruders dishonoured by their ignorance or their vices. The ewes have changed fold, and have no longer been fed in the same pastures; the holy churches have been abandoned; a frightful schism has divided the most beautiful kingdom in Europe; the father is armed against the son, the daughter against the mother, the husband against the wife; all sentiments of tenderness and confidence have been stifled; great scandals have afflicted pious souls; the persecution has reached the most respectable personages; the asylums of religion and virtue have been violated; they have played with the modesty of the weaker sex; the laws of honour and honesty have been violated. The National Assembly had knowledge of it, and did not repress these disorders; it has been accused, with justification, of having excited and authorised them, and of having covered the countryside with the ashes of the castles of those who denied it their applause; it did not prevent the blood of citizens from flowing.

It has covered under her aegis only the Protestants, the Jews, the Deists, the Freemasons, the philosophers: all the others have been persecuted. It has stripped the churches consecrated to the true

God; it has diminished their number; it has installed there, with armed force, ministers whom religion and virtue disavowed; it has permitted irreligion to be professed in her presence, and to borrow its language; it has even ordered that the honours of the religion of the true God should be granted to those who had blasphemed His holy name, or who had made fun of His immutable decrees.

A conduct so analogous to that of the Freemasons, and so conformable to their principles, evidently announces that their only object is to destroy the Christian Religion; that the National Assembly supports them with all its authority to succeed in them, and to substitute instead an emblematic religion, which unites all the sects; and which proposes to subject the whole universe to the system it professes, and which we find in the different degrees it has conjured up, to impose more easily on men who let themselves be taken in by the eyes, while the adepts, contenting themselves with a metaphysical religion and rising above modes and forms, adore in God only an abstract being without reality, in whom, following the lessons of the divine Plato, they bring together all the attributes we conceive of in Divinity. This great discovery differs from Spinoza's system only in the manner in which it is presented; as to substance, it is absolutely the same thing, since they both lead to atheism.

CHAPTER VI

Freemasonry Wants to Establish the Natural Religion

ever have Freemasons shown more indifference to Religion than today; Jew, Protestant, Lutheran, everything is allowed in their society, deists, even atheists are not excluded. The religion they profess accommodates all systems, extends to all individuals, and adopts, without repugnance, all the reveries of paganism. To give an authentic proof of it, it would be necessary here to analyse Masonic maps, which contain all that Plato, Manes, Pythagoras, the rabbis, the Gnostics have imagined on the origin of beings; on the perfections of God; on the active and passive powers of the sun and the moon, of man and woman, which are the emblem of nature; on the origin of ideas; on the manner in which abstractions are formed, and we would have, in evidence, the present philosophical system, the ideal world, on which is founded the irreligion of our days, and which will soon lead us to annihilate all idea of God, all feeling of piety, and even every kind of religion. For I claim that when we are in full agreement with Spinoza's system, such as our philosophers have worked it out, there will be no religion except for weak souls. But while waiting for this secret science to be brought to light, let us reveal a great Masonic truth, which we communicate to the followers, whose strength of spirit we have tested. We will see, in the degree of the Sun, that to lead to irreligion and the abolition of all worship, Freemasonry recommends only the Natural Religion. It will be easy to compare, if you will, the principles of Masonry with those of the Socinians, and to see their agreement.

DEGREE OF THE *CHEVALIER DU SOLEIL*

The lodge of the *Chevalier du soleil* must be lighted by only one light, since there is only one from which the world draws its brightness, just as there is only one lodge which is that which Adam received from God.

These principles are Socinian: heretics reject the inspiration of the Holy Spirit, the manifestation of the divine Word, and recognize only one

God, represented by one single light. The lodge that God gave to Adam is the whole world.

In this degree, the master is called Adam; the master of ceremonies who takes the place of overseer is called *Verité*,[1] the brothers are called Cherubim. Aprons are not worn. Adam carries a sceptre, at the end of which is a globe, because he was constituted as the first king of the created world, and father of all men. *Verité* bears a white rod, at the end of which is a golden eye; and next to his necklace, a white cord from right to left, at the end of which hangs, from a rosette, a golden eye; the jewel of the order is a necklace, from which hangs, from a golden chain, a golden sun, in the middle of a triangle of the same metal.

To open the lodge, Adam asks Brother Vérité what the weather is like.

Answer. It is midnight on earth, and the sun is at noon in this lodge.

Here is a very flattering answer for those who are not Freemasons; they are in darkness, while the light shines like noon in the lodge.

Adam says: Let us take advantage, my brothers, of the favour that this Supreme Being does us by enlightening us, to be able to lead us in the path of truth, by following the law which the Lord has engraved in our courses, which is the only one by which we can come to know the pure truth.

Like the Socinians, he wants to persuade fellow Masons that they only depend on a single Su-

---

1   French: Truth.

preme Being, who has given them no rule of conduct other than natural law. By this means, they exclude any submission to the Church, to any civil authority, paternal and ecclesiastical.

Then the master makes the sign to all the brothers, which is to put the right hand on the heart: all the brothers respond to it by raising the index finger of the right hand towards the sky, to mark that there is only one God, who is the force, father of the truth.

RECEPTION

The candidate presents himself alone at the door, his eyes bandaged with black crape, to mark the depth of the darkness by which he is surrounded; he gropes for some time before he finds the door. He strikes six blows with the flat of his hand, to designate the six days that preceded the creation of man. Brother Vérité, without opening the door, asks the candidate what he wants,

Answer. To see the light of truth; to rid me of the old man; to destroy in me the childish prejudices of error and falsehood, into which men have fallen by cupidity and pride.

Natural light is here in opposition to the light of the word of God, which enlightens every man coming into the world. The body of the old man should be understood as the character of the Christian; and the childish prejudices of error are the mysteries of revealed religion, sources of error according to the Socinians.

Adam orders Brother Vérité, to introduce the candidate to the centre of true happiness; *that is to say, inside the lodge.*

Brother Vérité opens the door, takes the candidate by the hand and leads him into the middle of the sanctuary, where the picture of happiness is drawn, covered with a black carpet. When he arrives there, Adam says, 'My son, since by your work in the royal art of Masonry, you have come to the point of desiring to know the truth, it must be shown to you quite naked. Consult yourself at this moment; see if your will is strong enough to obey it in everything it orders you. If you are at this moment as I desire, I am sure it is already in your heart, and that you must feel some movements that were previously unknown to you; if so, you must expect it will manifest itself before long. But beware of coming to defile its sanctuary by a pure spirit of curiosity, and beware of coming to increase the number of the profane; *that is to say, Christians*, who mistreated it for so long, that they forced it to conceal itself, and no longer to appear on Earth except under a thick veil. *Here is what forced the Socinians to surround themselves with emblems, in order to avoid the prosecutions that have been made against their persons.* However, it has never ceased to manifest itself in all its glory, and to show itself openly to true Masons. You have it in your heart, it is enclosed there by the worldly fear that has bound its hands and feet; I hope you will be a most intimate favourite. The ordeals through which you have passed guarantee me what I should expect from your zeal; thus, so that nothing is hidden from you, I order Brother Vérité to instruct you in what you need to know in order to attain true happiness.'

After Adam has finished speaking, the candidate's eyes are uncovered, and he is guided through the lodge without explaining anything to him. Then Brother Vérité speaks to him in these terms:

'My dear brother, the divine truth speaks to you through my mouth. Said truth has demanded of you trials with which it is satisfied. It has made you acquainted, by placing them in the order of Masonry, several of its creeds that, without its help, would still be for you natural enigmas from which you would not be able to derive any salutary fruit; but since you have been lucky enough to be admitted into this brilliant abode, learn that the first three items that you knew, such as the Bible, the compass, and the square, have a hidden meaning that you do not know.

'1°. By the Bible, you must understand that you must have no other law than that which Adam had at creation, and which the Eternal engraved on his heart. This law is what is called natural. You must worship and admit only one God.'

When a Mason therefore says that he accepts the Bible, that means, in the sense of the Socinians, that he accepts it as the language of natural law, and not as a divine work, nor as contain-

ing divine truths added to the general precepts of nature; therefore a Mason cuts out the mysteries from Holy Scripture, or interprets them only according to right reason. If he says that he adores and admits only one God, it must be understood that he does not adore the Son of God, nor the Holy Spirit; because according to the Socinians they are not God in the same sense as the Supreme Being. Jesus Christ, according to them, is only God because he was filled with the power and the power of God; but he is not so by nature, and therefore not consubstantial with his father. It follows from this that we must not honour the Blessed Virgin nor the Saints; and that was the great doctrine of Cagliostro, which he preached in all the lodges, which must have made him dear to the Protestants.

'2°. By the compass you must understand all that God has made and created is good; that he has nothing to do with the effect of chance.'

This doctrine makes no mention of the original sin which has vitiated our nature, and even seems to exclude it.

'With a compass, we form a circle, all the points of the circumference of which are equally distant from the central point. This is why this compass warns you that God is the central point of all things, both of which are equally near and equally distant from this All, which is God.'

Here is a very interesting discovery for the human race, and which reminds us of the systems of Hobbes and Spinoza. The good and the wicked are equally near or far from God; so there is no difference between good and evil other than that which ignoramuses attribute to it. The Freemasons, who have kept this doctrine hidden for so long, well deserve a reward for having finally brought it to light.

'3°. Through the square it is discovered to us that this same God has made all things equal; because the property of the square is to assure itself, by its means, of the perfect square; so the will of God, in creating the world, could only act in one way, which is that of perfect good.'

Here the established optimism and an imaginary equality.

'4°. Through the level, you will learn to be upright and firm, not to let yourself be carried away by the crowd of the ignorant and the blind; but to maintain in an unshakable manner the rights of natural law, and the pure and clear knowledge of the holy truth.'

Who would believe that the Freemasons' level is the emblem of the stubbornness of these gentlemen to maintain that natural law alone is preferable to all that pleased the word of God, and His spirit, to reveal to men? There is no need for astonishment; stubbornness is the nature of heresy. Insults and rudeness cost these gentlemen nothing when it is a question of rendering contemptible those who do not think like them. Ignorance and blindness are for the profane, and for the Freemasons alone the light of pure truth.

'5°. By the plump rule and the rough stone, you must understand the coarse man purified by reason, and perfected by the excellence of my master, truth.

'6°. The cubic stone means that all your actions must be equal in relation to the sovereign good.

'7°. The tracing board reminds you that you have a reason which must serve you to trace fair and well-proportioned ideas.

'8°. The columns remind you to be firm and steadfast when the truth has spoken to us and strives to become the ornament of the Masonic order.'

According to this Socinian system, we do not need to have recourse to Jesus Christ, *to his grace, nor to his mediation to do good; it suffices, for a Freemason, to cast his eyes on his tracing board, on the columns Jachin and Boaz; with this specific it must never fail.*

'9°. The blazing star, carried into the sanctuary where the ark is enclosed, warns you that the heart of a true Mason must be like a sun that shines in the darkness, and enlightens his brothers by its example.

'10°. The death of Hiram and the change of the master's word teach you that it is difficult to escape the traps that ignorance sets every day for the most virtuous men; but that it is necessary to show oneself as firm as was our venerable Hiram, who preferred to be massacred rather than yield to the persuasion of his assassins. You must live and die to uphold the rights by which the sovereign good is acquired.'

We see here why they now take the oath to win or die. They must defend the truth that they have sworn at the risk of our lives. The death of Hiram and that of the Grand Master of the Templars are great models for Freemasons.

'11º. The changing of the word holy to profane in the search of our reverend father Hiram means that vulgar ignorance does not stop at vile and superfluous words, which have only the prejudice of error and falsehood as their foundation, and which obtain credence and belief only from mysteries similar to those of the ancient Egyptians, and upon a tradition which has been changed from one century to another.'

This is how the Freemasons, in a convoluted style, seek to decry the tradition of the Catholic Church, its mysteries, and the Christian faith, by confusing the sacred with the profane, the sources created by tradition with the ridiculous symbols of the Egyptians.

'12º. You have gone through the degree of perfect master, you have seen there a pit, a corpse, a rope to pull it out and put it in the sepulchre, made in the shape of a pyramid, at the top of which is a triangle, in which is enclosed the name of the Lord. By the pit and the corpse, you must understand Man in the state in which you were before having had the happiness of knowing our order. The cord, with which the corpse is tied in order to remove it, is the bond of our order which has drawn us from the bosom of ignorance to arrive at the celestial abode where truth resides. The pyramid represents the true Mason who rises by degrees to the highest heaven, there to adore the sacred and unalterable name of the Eternal.'

Who would have thought that a Freemason was a pyramid? What a detour to teach us that a true Mason elevates himself, by means of the degrees he receives, to the highest of heavens, to adore there, not the Supreme Being, in whom a perfect Mason does not believe, but only his name, which is the emblem of the divine Being, which suffices for a Mason! It is clear that a good Mason does not believe in the Sacraments of the Catholic Church to sanctify himself, since his degrees take their place. That, then, is all, the religion of a Mason.

'13°. In the degree of English master and Parisian master, you saw a blazing star, a great candelabrum with seven branches, altars, vessels of purification, a great brazen sea.

By this degree you must understand that one must be cleansed of prejudice before passing into other degrees; to feel able to support the brilliant lights of reason enlightened by the truth, of which this light is the emblem.

By the seven-branched candelabrum you must hear the mysterious number of the great royal art, in which seven brothers together can initiate a layman who desires to come out of darkness, and impart to him the seven gifts of the spirit that will soon be known to you, when you will have been washed in the great brazen sea, and thereby purified.

You saw a small hanging chest, a key, a scale, and a burning urn.

This degree reveals that you must combat your prejudices and your passions, and that you must be a severe judge of them.

By the chest, we indicate the greatest observance of the secret that you must keep in your heart and cover with a black veil, that is, to ensure that the profane never have the slightest bit of knowledge of it.

By the key, you are warned to close your heart to all that is contrary to reason enlightened by the torch of truth; you are given to understand that you already know a part of our mysteries, and that by behaving with zeal and equity towards your brothers, you will soon come to know the general good of society.

The scales and the flaming urn represent to you that when you have reached the sublime knowledge of the order, you must, by your morals and your works, leave behind you, in the minds of your brothers, and even the profane, a lofty idea of your virtue, and make it so that it is perceived from afar, as one follows the odour of an urn filled with perfumes. This urn is flaming in the rank of the great Scotsman.

14°. Finally, you have seen many things which are repetitions of what you have already gone through. However, you will add three SSS to it, enclosed in a triangle; the planet of Mercury; the third chamber called Gibeon; the spiral staircase; the Ark of the Covenant; Hiram's Tomb; opposite the ark, the figure of Solomon, and the representation of the two columns of Jachin and Boaz.

By the three SSS, we mean the three main attributes of the Eternal, namely: knowledge, wisdom, holiness. The seven degrees made in outline, represent the different grades by which you must pass to reach the height of the glory represented by the word Gibeon, where you once sacrificed to the Most High, and whereupon having reached it, you must sacrifice your passions to do nothing except what will be prescribed by our laws.

Gibeon is mentioned here only as an emblem, for no more sacrifices have been made there than in all the high places, where the idolaters offered sacrifices to their gods. Gibeon was the capital of the Gibeonites, located on the top of a hill; it is, without doubt, because of its situation, or because of the word gabaa, *which, in Hebrew, means* hill, *that the Freemasons chose this emblem to designate a place where it is necessary to sacrifice; but it must be remarked that the pinnacle of glory to which a Mason must desire to attain is Masonic perfection, the laws of which must be the supreme rule of all the actions of a perfect Mason.*

The planet of Mercury is a sign of defiance to warn you to flee from those of your brothers who, by a false practice, maintain commerce with people of bad life, and who, more often than not, feign absence at our most sacred mysteries; that is to say, to flee those who, through a worldly fear, see themselves ready to deny their engagements.

One learns in Masonry to dissimulate, and to live with cowardly Masons as among enemies. We could perhaps ask, what is there in the mysteries of the order that is so holy and so respectable so as to exercise such rigorous severity towards those who refuse to assist in them?

The ark at the foot of which you have arrived, teaches you that having arrived in the holy of holies, you must no longer retreat, but rather perish to support glory and the truth, as did our reverend father Hiram, who deserved to be buried there.

Would a lodge of Freemasons be the emblem of heaven, and would one have acquired sovereign bliss when one had the privilege of entering the interior of a lodge? It must be admitted that if this is so, the Freemasons give us a strange idea of bliss. How many absurd ideas contained in three lines! Hiram being the figure of Jesus Christ, *it follows, according to the Freemasons, that this divine Saviour gave his life only to support the glory and the truth which one obtains when one has arrived at the holy of holies of a lodge; every Freemason must do the same, and this is where all these efforts must lead. Doesn't that lead to destroying the reality of an afterlife?*

Solomon exhorts you, by his zeal for the royal art, to follow the sublime career of the order of which he is the teacher.

Solomon is here only an emblem of Jesus Christ, *who, by his wisdom, established the priesthood, of which the Freemasons claim to possess among them the continuity without interruption, since* Jesus Christ, *the first Scotsman.*

The columns of Jachin and Boaz teach you, by their height and their beautiful proportions, to perform celestial actions among men capable of entering the path of truth.

15°. By the degree of favourites, you have understood the two kings who kept promises and alliances; the regrets they had for the loss of their cousin, and for the abuse of his graces.

This is an impious irony of the conversation of Moses and Elijah with Jesus Christ *on Tabor. These two prophets are treated as kings, because they had received the anointing which makes kings and prophets;* Jesus Christ *is treated as their cousin, because they had received, like him, the divine power and virtue, although with less abundance; it is in this sense that the Freemasons, the Socinians, and the Quakers call themselves children of God and his ministers.*

16°. In the grade of elected master, you must have noticed that of all the favourites who were in Solomon's room, there were only nine who were destined to avenge the death of our reverend Father Hiram; that is to say, in explaining the enigma to you, that many profane people have the good fortune to enter our sanctuaries; but very few are fortunate enough to come to know the sublime truth. If you ask me what qualities a Mason must have to arrive at the centre of true good? I will answer you that to arrive there, it is necessary to have crushed the head of the serpent of worldly ignorance; having shaken off the yoke of childhood prejudices concerning the mysteries of the dominant religion of the country where one was born. All religious worship was invented only by the hope of commanding and occupying the first rank among men, only by a laziness which engenders, by a false piety, the cupidity of acquiring the goods of others; finally, that by gluttony, daughter of hypocrisy, which makes use of everything to contain the carnal senses of those who possess it, and who constantly offer it, on an altar erected in their hearts, holocausts which voluptuousness, lust, and perjury procured for them.

It is by such speeches that they manage to pervert weak souls, to inspire the greatest contempt for the ministers of Religion, for Religion itself, and to pervert all of Holy History. The nine masters who come out of Solomon's room are the apostles, whose number they did not want to specify, the better to obscure history. They left the society of Jesus Christ *to go and avenge his death by the announcement of his glorious resurrection; but the Freemasons do not mention this path; it does not fit their system. They arrived at*

94

the sovereign good, not like the Freemason, but by crushing the head of the infernal serpent, and establishing, in all places, the Religion of Jesus Christ *on the ruins of idolatry. A Mason who does not believe in original sin, claims that the story of the serpent leaving Eve must be understood in a figurative sense, and that all the ministers of the Religion of* Jesus Christ *are impostors and ambitious; consequently, that the mysteries of Religion are phantoms, with which one stuns the ignorant. One could hardly explain oneself more clearly regarding the hatred that Masons have focused onto the Christian Religion.*

That, my brother, is all that which you must know to fight and destroy within you before you aspire to know the true good; here is the monster, under the figure of the serpent, which you have to exterminate. It is the faithful depiction of what the vulgar imbecile adores under the name of religion.

Can one teach more evidently and more energetically, that to become a perfect Mason, one must become an apostate from the Catholic Religion, deny all the mysteries, and renounce all the practices that Jesus Christ *has approved?*

Hiram was the truth on Earth, Abiram was a monster produced by the serpent of ignorance, who knows today how to set up altars in the heart of this timid profane. It is the same feared profane who, having become, by fanatical zeal, the instrument of monastic and religious rites, gave the first strokes in the bosom of our father Hiram; that is to say, sapped the foundations of the celestial temple to sublime virtue which the Eternal Himself had raised on Earth.

From this explanation it follows that Jesus Christ *was the truth on Earth; but that profane ignorance, represented by the person of Abiram, son of Hiel of Bethel, who perished when his father undertook to rebuild Jericho, introduced the ritual and the religious ceremonies, found only in Freemasonry, that put* Jesus Christ *to death.*

The first age of the world witnessed what I say. The simplest law of nature made our first fathers the happiest mortals. The monster of pride appears on Earth; he shouts, he makes himself heard by men and by the happy mortals of that time; he promises them beatitude, and makes them feel, by honeyed words, that it is necessary to render to the Eternal, creator of all things, a worship more marked and more extensive than that which had hitherto been practiced on Earth. This hundred-headed hydra deceived and deceives again and again the men who are subject to its empire, and will deceive them until the moment when the true elect will appear to fight it and entirely destroy it.

To understand this tirade, we must understand the Masons as the true elect, and the Catholic Church as the hundred-headed hydra of superstition.

17°. The great Scotsman, through the three degrees you have gone through, has taught you things that lead him to true good. Such is this great circle, which represents the immensity of the Supreme Being, which never had a beginning, and which will never have an end. The large triangle is the mystical figure of the Eternal. The three letters G, S, U, depicts for you various things. The first signifies the grace of the Masonic order; the second, submission to the same order; the third, union among the brothers who, all together, must form only the same body, or figure equal in all its parts, like the equilateral triangle.

The large letter G, in the middle of the triangle, means God or God, in English; it is placed in the middle of the triangle, to give to understand that each true brother must have engraved it at the depths of his heart. In this degree it is said that you have been received into the third heaven; that is to say, where pure truth resides, since it abandoned the earth to the monsters that persecute it. The end of the degree of Great Scotsman is a preparation to become more enlightened, to arrive at the entire knowledge of the true good. Also you see in this degree the baptism of the Syrian John the Baptist; that is to say, the true Mason, by the celestial light and by the renunciation of all worship, except that which admits only one God, creator of all things, adored in his tributes.

This doctrine must appear very dreadful to true Catholics; but at least it gives us the key to the whole system of Freemasonry, and the reason for the persecution experienced by the worship of the true God. We see how our religious principles are slandered, travestied and rendered contemptible in the eyes of the French youth who allowed themselves to be perverted. I spare the reader the rest of this degree so as not to bore him.

I know that the Freemasons repeat everywhere that they respect Religion, that they do the acts, etc. But I have only one observation to make to them, which is that all the religious instruments they have only remind one of a figurative religion; which has no real object, and which is therefore only adopted to impress the eye. But the speeches, the Masonic interpretations, tend only to destroy the foundations of revealed Religion, to substitute therein I don't know what religious emblems, the true explanation of which is almost never given to the candidates. We must look for it in Plato, in the history of the Socinians, in that of the Quakers, in the works of our philosophers, in the discourses of a certain world spoiled by philosophy, which hopes for nothing after death. The very works presented to the National Assembly often offer the same principles, and the manner in which they are received, leads one to believe that this august Assembly does not see with a bad eye that they are growing among the people.

Sometimes the providence of things is advocated; sometimes that religion consists only in morality; that a universal religion must be adopted; that it is necessary bring great men together, *whatever their opinions. In the memoir presented on the changes to be made in the new church of Sainte-Geneviève, the author says:* 'The pediment released from the insipid cluster of clouds, angels, and rays that only offend reason, would receive the image of the fatherland dressed in a long robe.' *However, this author, whose reason is offended to see angels, consents to put demons under the hands of the country. This change, it must be admitted, feels otherworldly. The haut-reliefs that memorialise Sainte-Geneviève saving Paris and feeding its inhabitants no longer have anything that interests him; he prefers vague ideas, aimless moralities, to paying, through recognition, for benefits received.*

On the summit of a monument consecrated to the great men of the country, *our author does not wish to allow the symbol of the Christians' faith to subsist; all that harks back to the idea of Religion must be effaced: it is necessary to put in its place the colossal statue of liberty or Fame. Nothing pleases him so much as the rights of man, nature based on equality and liberty, the happiness of the countryside, the wealth of the cities, the tranquillity of the empire; he would like to represent them everywhere under emblems. We see from this the taste of the public, our religious progress and all we owe to Freemasonry, which should grandly figure in such a beautiful monument, and where it has assigned the place for its great men.*

In the explanation of the lodge, attention should still be paid to a few emblems that give the key to the morals of the Freemasons.

The sun represents the unity of the Supreme Being.

The three SSS signify that only science, adorned with wisdom, makes man holy.

The three candelabra represent the course of human life, illuminated by the light of truth.

The four triangles show us the four main duties of the quiet life, 1º. brotherly love and the community of goods; 2º. all mysteries; 3º. not to do to others what we would not like done to us; 4º. to expect everything with confidence from the Creator, when we pass into the next life.

The seven planets represent the seven passions of life, useful to man when he knows how to use them with moderation; but when we abandon ourselves to them too much they become mortal sins, because they deprive us of a life that we must preserve in relation to God, who is its principle, and in whose eyes nothing is more criminal than to destroy the most precious of His works.

The seven cherubim represent the seven delights of life, which are smell, sight, taste, touch, rest, and health.

The reception represents the purity of nature, in that the views and intention of the Supreme Being are found fulfilled, having created men only for this end, according to these words addressed to Adam; Grow and multiply.

The Holy Spirit, represented by the dove, represents the figure of our soul, which being a breath of the Supreme Being, cannot be defiled by the works of the body, and is always ready to return to its whole, of which it is only part.

The temple represents our body, which we must take care to preserve.

The figure at the entrance to the temple tells us that we must watch over our needs, like a shepherd over his flock.

The columns, Jachin, Boaz, show us the firmness of soul that we must have in the good and the bad that happens to us in this life.

The seven degrees of the temple indicate the different degrees through which one passes before arriving at the knowledge of sovereign temporal happiness, which leads to spiritual.

The terrestrial globe is the figure of the world we inhabit.

Lux è tenebris, means that the enlightened man of reason has no trouble penetrating the darkness of ignorance and superstition.

The flame that crosses the globe represents the usefulness of the passions necessary to man in the course of life, as the waters are useful to the earth to make it fruitful.

The cross surrounded by serpents signifies that one must respect vulgar prejudices, and be careful not to show the bottom of one's heart in matters of religion.

These maxims are convenient; but very different from the morality of Jesus Christ.

The Freemasons have yet another way of explaining their signs, which recalls everything to matter, and suits alchemists and those who are at the head of the invention of the philosopher's stone.

The sun represents the unity of the Supreme Being, the one and only subject of the great work of philosophers.

The three *SSS*, *stellatus sedes solis*.

The three candelabra, the three degrees of fire that must be given to matter.

The triangles, the four elements, air, water, fire, and earth.

The seven planets, the seven colours which appear during the reign.

The seven cherubs, the seven metals, gold, silver, copper, iron, lead, tin, and mercury.

The design represents the purity of the material, so that it may keep spotless at the power of the king, whose name is *Albraes*.

The dove or the Holy Spirit represents the universal Spirit who gives life to all beings in the three kingdoms of the great work, the vegetable, the mineral, and the animal.

The entrance to the temple is represented by a body, because the nature of the great work is body; that is to say, the potable gold to be fixed.

The world represents matter.

The cross, the pains, and the works that must be endured to reach the last degree of perfection.

The caduceus is the double mercury that must

be drawn from matter; that is to say, mercury fixes gold and silver.

Stibium, password of the philosophers, which means antimony, from which we get the alkest, called the great work, or work of the philosophers.

After this explanation, the box is closed.

Adam to Brother Vérité.

Brother Vérité, what progress are men making on Earth to arrive at true happiness?

Answer. All follow vulgar prejudices, very few combat them, and very few succeed in this holy place in knocking at the door.

Adam to all the brothers:

My brothers, let us go to go among men, try to impress on them the desire to know the truth.

The apostles of Propaganda have only fulfilled this mission very well.

CHAPTER VII

The Freemasons Want to Abolish the Ecclesiastical Hierarchy of the Catholic Church

ne could perhaps imagine why they persecute Catholic priests everywhere; why they say nothing to schismatics, to Protestants, to Jews etc? It is because Freemasons, regarding themselves as the true successors of *Jesus Christ*, aim to unite under their government all those who profess His religion, and to become the only doctors of the religion they desire men to adopt, as the only true one, the one that must become the sole religion of the human race. Now, the Catholic priests are those who have the greatest horror of this doctrine, and who are in the best position to discover its poison and to combat it; they must therefore be infinitely odious to Freemasons; and it is against them that they must direct all their blows. They have done and do so every day. After having deprived them of their places, their possessions, and all their temporal consolations, they have twenty times tried to drive them out of the kingdom for imaginary crimes. If they could not overcome them, it is because the Freemasons' behaviour seemed too revolting. The latter have at least succeeded in preventing the priests, in an infinity of places, from exercising the functions of their ministry, which they have devolved to men without morals, separated from the centre of Catholic unity, and who draw their authority only from the people or ministers without jurisdiction. This first step taken, it should soon put them in a position to carry out all the projects they have conceived.

If I had not feared boring the public, I would have brought to light the degree of Freemason ministers, or fully-fledged Masonic priests, in order to demonstrate to the most incredulous that the persecution by Freemasons of the Catholic clergy comes from their wish that there should be no more priests, or that there should only be those in their image. The Protestants choose their ministers; Freemasons choose and consecrate theirs; they want, by a continuation of their principles, that the French choose Masonic priests and pontiffs; soon they will want them consecrated. Give them the time, they will soon find the means.

The public has ignored until this day the purpose of the steps that have been taken; it is time to undeceive it, by making it see that it has been duped by heretics, fanatics, enemies the most declared of the Religion of *Jesus Christ*; and that in obeying them, it overthrows, without suspecting it, the true, the only divine Religion which *Jesus Christ* has established; and that it is guilty of the most horrible outrage. It follows the impulse of the Freemasons, and these are the most bitter enemies of *Jesus Christ*, of his Church, of his priesthood, and, consequently, of his Holy Religion. It will be convinced of what I say by casting a glance at the consecration of Masonic ministers, priests, and pontiffs, under the names of Apprentice, Fellow Craft, and Scottish Master.

Each order in Masonry has three degrees: that of Apprentice, Fellow Craft, and Master. It is the same with Freemason Scottism, under the names of Small, Great Architect, Scotman. The lodges are adorned as in the other orders, but with more pomp and magnificence; after the usual preparations, the candidate is made to swallow, in order to become a Scottish Apprentice, a mysterious concoction which is presented to him with a golden trowel. This concoction is a kind of libation made with flour, milk, oil, and honey. It is, the candidate is told, a portion of Hiram's heart; or to speak the language of the Manichaeans, whose madness they imitate, it is the spirit and soul of Hiram, which they strive to convey to the heart of our apprentice, by making him eat a concoction made with materials that can represent its softness, wisdom, and strength. It is from St Augustine that we learn this usage of the Manichaeans.

Animam verò bonampartem scilicet Dei, pro me ritis inquinationes suæ, per cibos etpotus in quibus anteà colligata est, venire in hominem; atque ità per concubitum carnis vinculo colligari. Augustinus cons trà duas epistolas Pelagii, lib. 4, cap. 6.

'Beausobre claims that this Manichaean system has been partly adopted by some modern scholars, who pass for the most profound philosophers of our century.' *Histoire des Manich.*, tom. II, book. 8, c. 4. §. 5.

At any rate, this Masonic preparation, which strongly smacks of metempsychosis, the powerful Master knows how very skilfully to use in making the candidate understand the mysterious union he contracts with spiritual Masonry: the effect that oil and wine must produce, to heal the wounds of his soul, as the good Samaritan did to heal the wounds of a man who had fallen into the hands of thieves. The milk and flour that constitute the first nourishment of children, announce to the candidate that, being only an apprentice, he is like a child to whom is given only gentle and easily digestible food.

However, before giving this concoction, the candidate makes his confession, according to the formula of the Protestants, which consists in promising to sin no more. 'I promise,' he says, 'on the same obligations that I contracted in the preceding degrees, and before this august assembly, to have, keep, and hide the secrets of the architects, never to reveal them to any brother of the inferior degrees, or to the profane, under pain of being deprived of the honourable burial granted to our respectable master; finally, I promise to support Masonry with all my strength, and to assist, as much as I can, all my brothers.'

Then the powerful Master takes the golden trowel, which is in the urn, covers it with mystical paste, and presents it to the mouth of the candidate, to swallow some, saying to him: 'Let this mystical paste that we share with you, forms forever a bond so indissoluble, that nothing is able to break it; say with us, as well as all the brothers: Woe to him who divides us.'

When the candidate returns to his place, in the most respectable manner for the assembly, the Very Powerful says to him: 'My brother, what you have just done teaches you that you must never refuse to make the confession of your faults, that obstinacy and stubbornness must be banished from the heart of every good Mason.'

We can conclude from this instruction that in the judgment of Freemasons sins are revoked by this mysterious concoction. It would be interesting to learn wherefrom it derives this virtue.

It is about, after that, making the Scottish Apprentice participate in the spirit of *Jesus Christ*; we try it, by turning him face down; so that he is on his hands and knees, his face on the flaming letter, and his mouth glued on the letter god, engraved on a golden triangle plate. Then come the journeys, after which the signs and secret grips are given, along with the cord, the jewellery, the gloves, and the apron.

DEGREE OF SCOTTISH FELLOW CRAFT.

When the above degree has been given, one proceeds to the following one, which is that of Scotch Fellow Craft; the reception of this degree becomes more interesting: however, I will not describe it in full yet. It suffices to know that the second drapery red, sprinkled with hyacinth flowers, and that on the altar are placed eighty-one lights, with all the attributes of the worship of the Old Testament. We see a transparent picture, representing the glory of the great Architect, surrounded by seven celestial intelligences. In the middle of the luminous triangle is the name of *Jehovah* written in Hebrew. The Ark of the Covenant is covered with the wings of Cherubim; the lamb of life rests on a book with seven seals; the sea of air is supported by twelve golden oxen; the ten urns are ranged on both sides of the altar; next to it is the candelabrum with the seven branches, the altar of the holocausts, the showbread.

The master of ceremonies makes the candidate understand that he is destined to replace Hiram. It's the reason why they gather all the figures of the Old Testament, symbols of the old covenant, which had their fulfilment in *Jesus Christ*, in order to make the candidate understand, in a more sensitive way, that he is going to be prepared for this performance. Now, if the Scottish Fellow Craft represents *Jesus Christ*, he is, like him, the temple of the true religion, since it is said in the Apocalypse that in the new Jerusalem, of which St John makes the description in chapter 21, there is no temple, because the Lord God Almighty and the lamb are his temple. It is for this reason that when the Scottish Fellow Craft is received, he is told that the temple is made.

The Scottish Fellow Craft having become, by his reception, the successor of Hiram, he is given the name of *Moabon*, which means son of my father, to show that all masons are brothers, and descendants of the same father, Hiram. Here is the new succession, and the new generation of pontiffs of Masonry, the new tribe of Levi, whose ministry can be established in the whole universe, this grand lodge where all the true friends of the Masonic creed must gather.

DEGREE OF SCOTTISH MASTER

We will stop in this degree only at the points most able to make us notice the spirit which reigns there.

ARRANGEMENT OF THE LODGE

The tomb of Hiram is placed between four aca-
cias, a death's head is added in representation at
the head of the tomb, two bones in saltire, and a
few teardrops scattered over the tomb; the lodge is
meant to represent Solomon's temple. The West,
which is supposed to be the vestibule, is draped in
white; the tomb of Hiram is in the middle, raised
from the ground about two feet; in the tomb, is a
golden triangle. The East of the lodge is draped
in red and represents the holy of holies. A glory is
placed at the bottom, in the middle of which, in a
triangle, is the holy name of God in Hebrew, etc.

The brothers have their hats on, their bare
swords in their left hand, the point turned towards
the tomb, the right hand ready. They bear crapes,
and they speak in feigned pain. Between the throne
of the Very Powerful there should be two dais, one
above the tomb from which hangs the golden triangle, the other above the two overseers. The Very
Powerful is guarded by two brothers, unsheathed
swords in hand; the lodge is superbly lit, and there
are eighty-one candles on the altar.

The opening of the lodge begins with a prayer,
which is as follows:

'Great Architect of this vast universe, leave your
celestial abode, preside over us today, and deign
to enlighten our works, so that we can imitate
your designs which you delineated formerly to our
first Masons, who worked to build edifices to ex-

alt your glory: direct the workers you employ; may our works be as solid as your duration, as closed as your designs, as great as your power. Guide us with your wisdom, restrain us with your justice; fill us with zeal to fulfil our duties, with fervour for our sacred mysteries, with firm constancy in our troubles; shed on us your precious lights, that our works never deviate from the limits that you have prescribed for us: that our hearts are always pure, that they are an agreeable offering to you; and may our troubles make us all worthy of working one day in the lodge of lodges, which is the reward of all good Masons. So be it.'

The candidate having entered the lodge with the customary ceremonies; the Very Power-ful makes him undergo an interrogation, which looks like a sacramental confession, and which is followed by the remission of faults.

The Very Powerful says: My dearest brother, does your conscience not reproach you for what you owe to Masonry?

Answer. No.

The Very Powerful. Are you guilty of some trea-son against our order, since you received the light?

Answer. No.

The Very Powerful. Have you always kept in your heart deep respect for all you owe to the great Architect of the universe, master of light?

Answer. Yes.

The Very Powerful. Has your conduct always been such that the divine precepts of our holy law have been the perfect model of your morals?

Answer. Yes.

The Very Powerful. Have you been faithfully submitted, in mind and heart, to the will of the august monarch who governs us?

Answer. Yes.

The Very Powerful. Have you let nothing of our holy mysteries slip out before the profane, either in jest or levity?

Answer. No.

The Very Powerful.[1] What would you have done if you had lived in the time of those three unfortunates who assassinated our respectable master; would you have avenged his death?

Answer. Yes.

The Very Powerful. Have you always been faithfully attached to the strict observance of the obligations which you have contracted before the great Architect of the universe?

Answer. Yes.

The Very Powerful. Have you ever found anything in our obligations which is contrary to the holy religion which we profess, or against the state, good morals, or ourselves?

Answer. No.

The Very Powerful. Do you intend to attain the degree of Scotsman?

Answer. Yes.

The Very Powerful. Will you always be faithful

---

1   In the original text, the words 'The Very Powerful', are missing in this and the next question. I have added them. —Ed.

to your commitments?

Answer. Yes.

The Very Powerful. Do you promise never to visit secret lodges?

Answer. Yes.

The Very Powerful. Will you always recognise in your brothers the virtuous men who will give you sufficient marks of their Masonic qualities?

Answer. Yes.

Speech in the Form of Exhortation

'Know, my very dear brother, so as never to forget it, that were tepidity or disgust for our holy mysteries to take hold of your heart, you would be all the more reprehensible, having received a more eminent light. Your crime would be notorious, being perfect Scots. Finally, you will see the end of Masonry, to which you will be more particularly attached by the narrow obligations you will contract. You will know our holy mysteries in all their extent; our brothers will become dearer to you; your needs will be theirs; for, do not doubt it, the strong must work for the weak. More human respect, more respect for persons, no more distinction, than that produced by virtue, it will no longer be in your power to renounce our particular acts of Masonic virtue, nor our holy libations!'

We see the spirit of Masonry in this piece; that is to say, a mixture of holy and profane ceremonies, a language modelled on the discourse of Je-

sus Christ *to his Apostles, on the day of the Last Supper, and an affectation not to say a word about Him, nor about the graces of the Holy Spirit, nor about the Church He sanctified.*

After the confession that the candidate has been made to undergo, he is told to withdraw for a moment and to collect himself as if to receive the absolution given after what Elisha says to Naamam: 'yourself and you will be purified.' Accordingly, the Very Powerful tells the candidate to wash his hands.

Then, they sent him on a voyage; he is given the signs, the word, and the grip, and the lodge begins to open. The Very Powerful takes great care to ask all the brethren if they consent to the candidate being introduced before them, to receive a new degree of light, and to admit him to the number of those who work to perfect the holy of saints.

Here is the form of reception that it is desired to introduce into the Catholic Church of France, and that the assembly has decreed.

The Very Powerful asks the candidate, what he desires? His answer is that he wants to acquire the mysterious knowledge of the holy of holies, and the mysterious word to make himself known to those who are admitted there, and to help them with zeal, fervour, and constancy.

This answer relates to the fable that the Rabbis made about the invention of the word Jehovah, with which Jesus Christ *must have done, according to them, mysterious things. It is according to* the same principles that Freemasons use the word Jehovah in all their consecrations.

Before giving this word to the candidate, the Very Powerful reminds him of Masonic morality which consists in loving good, fleeing evil, and practicing virtue.

After the journeys made, the Very Powerful says to the candidate: 'My brother, do you persist in your resolution?' The candidate answers, 'Yes,' and the Very Powerful man addresses him in a short speech.

'My brother, the voyages you have just made in the three enclosures mark the resignation of a good Mason who allows himself to be led, and who believes that all the symbolic ceremonies of our respectable order only tend to adorn it, by degrees, to receive the true light reserved for the beloved people of the great Architect of the universe. You have walked the temple enclosures; you are now in the place that represents the vestibule of the temple of Solomon, where the body of our respectable master was placed. Bow down before his tomb; you will receive the light to see the simulacrum of the monument that was raised, by order of Solomon, to honour the memory of the fairest of men.'

The Socinians and Freemasons call themselves the beloved people of God; what blasphemy! they make the candidate prostrate before the simulacrum of a man; what idolatry! what nonsense!

They show the light, the tomb, the triangle, etc.; and after this ceremony, the candidate makes his oath, and a vow, which probably does not resemble those that the assembly has just taken.

OBLIGATION

'On all the liberty that I profess in all the five natural senses, on the existence of my reason and my mind, which I declare to be in no way under subjection; on the intelligence which supports me, guides me and enlightens me, I promise, I swear, and I make a vow inviolably to keep all the secret signs, mysteries that have been unveiled to me until now and that will be revealed to me in the future, in the first five degrees of perfect Masons and of perfect Masonry, to which I am initiated; approving aloud and intelligibly and without fear, now that my life is free and my mind unpreoccupied, and that I have no regrets at having committed myself, though in the obscurity of our lodges; declaring them from my heart, and holding them inviolable, permitting, if I reveal them, that my body may undergo all the pains and rigors which commit me to it. May I open the veins of my temples and throat; and, exposed naked on the highest pyramid, may I be exposed to suffer, on this hemisphere, the rigors of the winds, the ardour of the sun, and the cold of the night; that my blood flows out slowly from my veins until the extinction of the spirit which animates the substance, the corporeal matter; and to increase the sufferings of the body and the spirit, that I be forced to take every day a

proportioned and sufficient nourishment, to pro-
long and preserve a devouring and cruel hunger;
there's nothing too rigorous for a perjurer. May
the laws of Masonry be my guides to guarantee me
and may the great Architect of the universe help
me. *Amen.*'

*We see clearly enough, without needing to say
it, how fanatical, impious, and cruel this oath
is; and therefore how much an august Assembly
ought to employ its authority to outlaw it: yet it
will do nothing.*

When the candidate has pronounced his oath,
the paper on which it is written is burned, and as
soon as it is consumed, three knocks follow.

After the customary proclamations, the Very
Powerful says to the candidate:

'My brother, since your zeal for Masonry has
induced you to persevere with firmness, we are
going to recognise you as superintendent of the
tabernacles which we erect. (These words, *intend-
ants*, *overseers*, are the equivalent of the word
bishop.) But first, let us render our homage to the
ghosts of our master, whose death we have hitherto mourned. Let our hearts be devoted to medi-
tation, and let our minds entertain his memory in
profound silence.' *This proves that Hiram is always regarded as dead and not risen.*

All the brothers, their knees on the ground, their
heads bent over their hands, remain silent. The
brother overseers have the candidate kneel before
a table, his head bent over the book on it, covering

his face with both hands, and the overseers cross their swords over his neck.

This attitude is very likely to give birth to deep ideas.

The drapery changes, everything is in red; the brothers put on their cord, and proclaim Moabon, successor of Hiram. A scale is placed in his hand; they lead him to the brazen sea, and pour water on his left side, and the Very Powerful says, 'Be cleansed.' While he is introduced into the most holy place, all the brothers come to order, knees on the ground, faces turned towards the sacred word of *Jehovah*, left hand on hip, in the shape of a triangle; and while the candidate meditates, the Very Powerful makes this prayer:

'O great Architect of the universe! you, whose holy and sacred name unites the workers scattered over the hemispheres to perfect the work of an edifice erected to celebrate you, deign to inspire us at this moment when we propose to associate this Mason with our work, and to make him participate in the advantages which are his reward. If he were capable of deceiving or betraying us, punish him yourself; may your thunderbolt annihilate him, may his name be withered, and his memory proscribed from age to age among the masons. O great Architect of the universe! you, whose holy and sacred name unites the workers scattered over the hemispheres, to perfect the work of a building erected to celebrate you, deign to inspire us at this moment when we propose to associate this Mason with our work, and to make him participate in the advantages which are his reward. If he were capable of deceiving or betraying us, punish him yourself; may your thunderbolt annihilate him, may his name be withered, and his memory proscribed from age to age among the Masons.'

This prayer finished, the Very Powerful takes fire and incense from the altar, and says to the candidate: 'My first brother, you have been purified by water; now I purify you with fire and incense. Remove iniquity and jealousy from your heart; always be pure in the eyes of the great Architect, etc.'

After that, the candidate having knelt on the south side, the Very Powerful blesses a vessel of oil, tracing on it, with a golden trowel, the word *Jehovah*. Then he takes this oil, and traces the same word *Jehovah* on the forehead, on the right eye and on the heart of the candidate, while pronouncing prayers.

PRAYER ON THE FOREHEAD.

'Great Architect, let this sacred mark be a proof that this brow will not henceforth blush before you, bearing the character of your divinity; never suffer your name to be profaned, and that head to be constantly filled with the same spirit that you once bestowed on the conductor of the beloved temple.'

PRAYER ON THE RIGHT EYE.

'May this eye, henceforth marked with your seal, no longer see anything but a pure light; pierce the tendencies which had obscured it, and make it see, in the darkest night, the cleared path that all good Mason must follow to arrive at the heavenly abode.'

PRAYER ON THE HEART.

'May this divine character, imprinted on your heart, warm it, kindle it and fill it with virtue. May zeal, fervour and constancy be forever the basis of your heart, purify it and keep it spotless, to be always worthy of being presented, as the most precious offering that can be made to you.'

PRAYER FOR COMMUNION.

After tracing *Jehovah*'s word on the bread, the Very Powerful says: 'Eat this, it is the reward of your labours, said the angel to the prophet Elijah, and do not forget that God does not abandon those whose actions are pleasing to him. It is in commemoration of the good deeds that every good Mason must do, that you eat this bread, my dear brother; and if you lack it, you will find brothers generous enough to share with you the reward which the great Architect of the Universe will have granted them. In this earthly lodge, no action could be more agreeable to him than this, since his son indicated it &

his disciples, according to the vulgar, on Maundy Thursday, and even since at Emmaus, after his resurrection.'

PRAYER WHEN DRINKING THE WINE.

'Drink this wine in commemoration of the use authorised by the great Architect of the Universe towards faithful servants, as Boaz towards Ruth. This action was most pleasing to the Lord; this is why we must admit into our meals the poor as well as the rich, as soon as they are virtuous; that's how the Scots do it these days.'

WHEN GIVING THE RING.

'Receive this ring as a token of the covenant you make with virtue.'

UPON BESTOWING THE CORD AND THE JEWEL.

The Very Powerful says: 'This cord and this jewel give you the command in chief over all the other Masons of the lower ranks'.

UPON BESTOWING THE GLOVES.

He says: 'These gloves belong to this degree. The first two words of this degree are *Urim* and *Thumim*. The word *Jehovah* is the ancient word of master, and the ineffable name of God, etc.'

These details suffice to prove that the degree of Scotsman is, among the Freemasons, a degree of ministers, who appear in lodges, like our priests and our pontiffs in the Catholic Church. All the ceremonies contain the principles of the Protestants and the Socinians. They do not recognise the authority of the Catholic Church; that is why they do not quote it. Nor do they invoke the grace or virtue of the Holy Spirit; they do not believe in it. All the sanctity of the ceremony depends on the virtue that they attach to the pronunciation of the word *Jehovah*, and this claim smacks of the rabbi and the Kabbalah. Enlightened men and fanatics have adopted it, because anything that strays from the Catholic rite is always in good taste; and however absurd it may be, it is always received as thanksgiving when it can be used to support a false opinion. In the *Last Supper*, there is only mention of commemoration according to Protestant principles. The end of all this heretical consecration is to give ministers to the lodges, and to dazzle the eyes of those present. It is the people who take part in this ceremony; nothing better suited to make it agreeable to them.

CONSEQUENCES OF THE MASONIC SYSTEM, WHICH EXPLAIN CURRENT EVENTS.

1°. Freemasons persecute the ministers of *Jesus Christ*, because they have renounced him; and they want, as far as He is in them, to take from Him

His divinity, His quality of Saviour and Redeemer of the human race, of Mediator between God and men, of Head of the Christian Church, and to force all those who profess this Doctrine to abandon it.

2°. The Freemasons, in the clubs, have concluded that it is necessary to close the churches of the Catholics, in order to prevent the worship which is rendered to *Jesus Christ*, and to substitute, in its place, the religion of the lodges, or a methodical irreligion.

3°. The Freemasons condemn the vows, and everything related to evangelical perfection, because this sublime doctrine is too superior to theirs, which flatters the passions, which they judge closer to the weakness of human nature, and which they would like, for this reason, so much to put in vogue, that it should be the only one in line on the globe, and become the universal religion.

4°. The Freemasons demand, with fury, the national oath, because it commits to schism and apostasy those who take it, and brings them closer to their society, into which they would like to include all men.

5°. They desire that the priests and the other ministers of the Catholic Religion no longer wear the habit of their rank except in the temples, when they are in office there; because this usage is established in their lodges, with regard to their ministers.

6°. They do the impossible no longer to pay them, although they have taken away their possessions or those that were intended for them; because their Scots receive no payment in the lodge for the exercise of the functions devolved to them.

7º. They are transported with a kind of fury against the priests, the monks, and even the nuns, whose number they would like to reduce; because this successive reduction will tend to the annihilation of the whole body, which prevents Freemasons from making themselves necessary, from dominating, and from establishing their opinions without contradictions and without obstacles.

8º. They have taken away, as much as it has been in their power, from secular and religious congregations, the books from which they could learn, in order to make them fall back into ignorance which alone can prevent them from speaking.

9º. They have, in several places, profaned the sacred vessels containing the holy hosts, because, according to the Protestant system which they have adopted, they do not believe in the real presence of *Jesus Christ* in the Eucharist, and they are happy to accustom Catholics not to believe in it, or to insult them in their belief.

10º. The profanation of Catholic temples by Freemasons should not astonish those who know that in their eyes there is no real sanctity, whether it lies only in opinion or in the imagination; this is why, in the ordination of the Scotsman, his hands are not blessed, they are only made to wash them as a sign of purity. All the sanctity of Masonic lodges and mysteries depends on the word *Jeho-*

vah which, being an abstract name, contains only an abstract idea that has no reality anywhere. It is with this word as with that of animal in general, of man in general, which does not exist. Thus *Jehovah*, signifying, in the Masonic sense, being in general, that which includes them all, that from which they derive their origin, presents to the imagination only a vague idea, similar to that which Spinoza had invented. It is, in the sense of the Freemasons, the soul of the world, the universal soul diffused through all, which animates and vivifies all, but whose substantial reality is not in any place. It is from this principle that our scholars conclude that there is no God to be feared after death, and that they are reassured about their future fate. The body, they say, falls into dissolution at death, and the soul unites with that universal soul, the assemblage of all the perfections, of which they regard theirs as forming a part. This system, so common today, is the overthrow of all religion and all moral sentiment; this is one of the reasons why we see so few morals today, such general selfishness, such great carelessness about one's future state, such great indifference for religion, such general relaxation in morals, such a studied search for the sweetnesses of the present life, such a universal abandon to carnal passions.

11°. It is therefore evident that it is to Freemasonry that the Church of France must impute the desolation to which it is reduced, the like of which is such as it has never experienced. Not content with attacking its mysteries, its doctrine, its faith, its maxims, it has loosened all the bonds of society, loosened all the springs of government, tried all means of perversion, and corrupted even the germ of good and virtue.

12°. The evil which Freemasonry has produced is so much the greater because it has left nothing untouched: as crime has become bolder and virtue more timid; children suck it almost with the milk; youth is more undisciplined; the principles of morals are received with more indifference, and teachers take less interest in teaching them, since their pupils have made a habit of infringing them.

13°. In such a general disorder, it is up to the Church of France to see, in its wisdom, what means it must employ to uproot its children from schism, from the oblivion of Religion, from heresy, from impiety and to all the crimes which defile the present generation, and which will extend their ravages to future generations.

14°. I could have unveiled all that Freemasonry has that is dangerous in its principles and maxims, and made known to all those who are involved in this famous order, how well they have made themselves criminals against God, against their country, against themselves; but at this moment, when one is inundated with pamphlets and papers, one cannot sustain the reading of a voluminous work. It suffices to have indicated the source of the evil; those who have participated in it can judge themselves in the tribunal of their conscience and prevent a more formidable judgment.

CHAPTER VIII

Freemasonry Wants to Overthrow the Throne, Like it Overthrew the Altar

I t is not only by its principles of liberty and equality, it is also by its actions and its undertakings of all kinds, that Freemasonry wishes to overthrow all authority not subject to its own; for the latter is well extended and very formidable. Although a Mason talks about nothig but freedom and equality, although he is made to give up all titles and all decorations and to content himself with the dear name of brother, in the lodge, when it convenes, he experiences all the rigor of despotism. The only thing that seems to soften him is the judgment of his brothers. When the Grand Master speaks, we must necessarily obey, or expect severe penance. But everything is sweet in the lodge, and coming from the venerable and very powerful master: everything is hard and unbearable coming from a king and a sovereign in his estates.

The Freemasons, who abolish all orders of national chivalry, do not touch those they have erected as Knights of Jerusalem, Knights of the East, Knights of the Sword, Knights Kadosh, Eagle Knights, Knights Templar. We feel the reason for it; they only disarm those whose resistance they recognise; they arm, on the contrary, those who can sustain their cause and defend their party. Wishing to destroy royalty, they broke all the bodies that seemed to support it; they attached contempt to all the rewards received for services rendered to the King; they have abolished the titles and honours that served to decorate the throne and to enhance its lustre; they chained the royal power; and if they grant the title of king to the supreme head of the nation, it is only as a title of office, such, more or less, as that of the Grand Master, which changes according to the degrees that he administers, and over which he presides; this title he draws from his brothers, who can deprive him of it by deposing it, or perpetuate it according to their will, but who is always dependent on the will of those who grant it. This is how they would wish the King to be king, a king of the theatre, by function, a removable king according to the will of those who would have chosen him; finally, to put it in two words, a Mason king.

Of all the orders of Masonic chivalry, that which seems to me the most dangerous is that of a Knight Templar or a Knight Kadosh; because he furnishes, in his misfortunes and principles, all that can animate a knight-Mason to revenge. The principles of this order are the same as those of Freemasonry, which some claim to have inherited from the Templar order; its misfortunes are also those of this order, which succumbed under the rigor of persecution, or rather of the punishment it was made to sustain for its crimes.

This order of the Templars had been founded in 1118, by Hugues de Payens, Godfrey of Saint-Omer, and seven other brothers, to defend Christian pilgrims against the cruelty of infidels. These knights made the three vows of chastity, obedience, and poverty at the hands of Warmund, patriarch of Jerusalem; and Baldwin II, king of this city, gave them a lodging near the temple, whence they took the name of Templars or Knights of the Temple. The Council of Troyes, in 1128, instructed St Bernard to give them a rule: he gave them that of St Benedict,[1] mitigated. Pope Eugene III, in 1146, ordered them to wear a red cross on their white habit. From that time, the number of the Templars, their houses, and their wealth increased considerably; but these riches became fatal to them. They were reproached with pride, avarice,

---

1   *The Rule of Benedict* is a book of precepts written in 516 by Benedict of Nursia (c. AD 480 – 550) for monks living communally under the authority of an abbot.

impurity, drunkenness: they were accused, in the ceremony of their reception, of renouncing *Jesus Christ*, of spitting on the cross, of worshiping the figure of the sun, and of kissing the Grand Master indecently in several parts of the body.

All these crimes were revealed by a knight named *Squin*, and Philippe-le-Bel, king of France, obtained from Bertrand de Got, pope under the name of Clement V, leave for proceedings to be taken against the Templars. The inquest began in 1306 and was continued throughout Christendom until 1312. The council of Vienna then pronounced the abolition of this order and forbade it to receive novices.

The Grand Master of the Templars was then Jacques de Molay; he first confessed, and then denied the corruption of his order. Some Templars agreed, and others persisted, even to the death, in denying all that was imputed to their order. Several were absolved, and others burnt. Their property was partly confiscated to indemnify the Catholic powers for the necessary expenses incurred to end this trial; and a great part of it was given to the Order of Malta.

The executions of the guilty began in France, and were continued in Spain, Italy, England, Germany, and Cyprus. However, not all the Templars were put to death; several held out for a time at Mayence and others retired to England, where the Freemasons pretend that they made proselytes under the name of Freemasons.

Although it is very difficult for them to make their affiliation to monuments certain and authentic, the destruction of this order excessively authorises them nevertheless to exact vengeance against the kings who have concurred in the judgment rendered by all the powers, in order to use it as a favourable opportunity to attempt the life of sovereigns, and to avenge, through the latter's deaths, a crime of which the latter are innocent, but which serves as a pretext for the Freemasons to satisfy the hatred they have conceived against them.

One reads, on one of the seals of the Baron de Menou, the motto of the league formed against throne and altar: it is conceived in these terms: *Enemies of worship and kings.* A chief of modern philosophers said, during his lifetime: *That the peoples would not be happy until the last of the kings had been strangled with the bowels of the last of the priests.* The maxims published today, and which everyone repeats at will, are *that men are equal; that none of them can be their superior, nor command them against their will; that all the peoples of the universe cannot belong to a handful of men who are the sovereigns; but that these must rather belong to the multitude; that it is up to the peoples to give and take back sovereignty according to their will.*

These seditious maxims could easily be stifled if no one was found in a position to uphold them with open force. It was therefore necessary, to give them efficacy, that there should be found knights who professed to defend them with arms. Now, it is in Freemasonry that this chivalric order was formed, and where they swear there to assassinate the kings of France and the popes.

Degree of Knight Kadosh or Templar

The lodge is tended in the same way as the chosen one of the nine. The reception of the candidate is done in a dark place by five brothers. There is a cave in which the bones of Grand Master Molay supposedly rest, accompanied by a lamp. The mannequin represents the person of the King of France who killed the Grand Master of the Templars on the scaffold. The candidate is stretched out on the ground like a corpse; in this attitude, he is made to repeat all the degrees he has received, and the oaths he has pronounced. A beautiful painting of this degree is made for him; which it is demanded of him never to bestow on a Knight of Malta. He is made to mount a double ladder, each rung of which represents one of the letters of the name of Philippe-le-Bel and that of Bertrand de Got. When he has reached the last rung, he is made to fall, to make him understand that he has arrived at the *nec plus ultrà* of masonry. They arm him with a dagger and make him thrust it into this prepared mannequin; and when the blood flows abundantly, the riddle is explained to him. The reward he is promised is his advancement in Masonry and the right to bear the arms of the Templars, the double cross, a spread eagle, holding a dagger in its claws.

The sign is to raise the right hand to the heart, then extend it horizontally and let it fall on the knee, to mark that the heart is disposed to vengeance. The grip is given by taking each other's hands as if to stab each other.

The technical words used are borrowed from the Hebrew, and designate that the profane has been killed, that he has been cut off from the number of the living.

CATECHISM

Question. Are you a knight?

Answer. Yes, I am, and my name is Chevalier Kadosh. *This Hebrew word means renewing; because the purpose of this degree is to renew the human race by making it pass from slavery to liberty. We have been enjoying this great advantage for two years.*

Question. Who received you?

Answer. A Deputy of the Grand Master.

Question. In which place?

Answer. In a deep cave, during the silence of the night.

Question. What do you pronounce coming from the cave?

Answer. Nekom. *This word means I killed him, cut him off from the number of the living.*

Question. What do you have in hand?

Answer. The traitor's head.

It is evident that it is from Masonry that has come to us the new invention of carrying in one's hand and showing to the public the head of the one who has been assassinated. Paris has often seen this spectacle, and even the provinces have not been deprived of it.

One must notice here a contradiction in the murdered person; his name is Hiram; instead, he should be called Molai. But this confusion of names has its utility in blurring ideas and saying whatever one wants; for it is good to observe that the Freemasons have borrowed from history facts by the aid of which they make understood all they wish. In the story of the death of Jesus Christ, it happens that those who contributed most direct-ly to his death are Judas, Caiaphas, and Pilate; that is to say, a Roman traitor, pontiff, and gov-ernor, who was as powerful as a viceroy. It is similar characters who contributed to the torture of the Grand Master of the Templars; a traitor, named Squin; a pontiff, Bertrand de Got; a king, Philippe-le-Bel. This comparison serves them to alter the history of the passion of Jesus Christ, and to confuse it with that of the Grand Master of the Templars.

Question. What reward are you hoping for?

Answer. The destruction of vice, the love and gratitude of my brothers. *It is by such hopes that fanaticism is sustained.*

Question. How do you name the workers who united for the construction of the new temple?

Answer. Paul-Kal, Pharas-Kal, *meaning those who put the profane to death. Which means that those who are thus united can become the murderers of all those who prevent them from raising the temple they have planned. It is today the conceit of Freemasons to be armed for the defence of each other; to form a numerous body spread over almost every place, but especially in the large towns; not to be destructible without depopulating the earth they inhabit, and to be assured that those who wish to alter their principles will risk seeing all their enterprises fail.*

Chapter IX

Conclusion

his outline of Freemasonry show the goal of this society, but it does not reveal all its vices; it would take several volumes to describe the indecency committed there, the errors confirmed there, the absurdities taught there. Sometimes we would see that it is the rendezvous of all pleasures, or the abode of the scoundrel and of the grossest impurity; sometimes we would witness ridiculous, comical, impious, and sacrilegious scenes.

A lodge is alternately a school of Stoic and Epicurean morality; fanaticism arms hands with daggers, and trains its adepts to commit crimes with unfailing intrepidity; the dreams of astrologers succeed the pretensions of alchemists, the opinions of pagan philosophers are associated with the delusions of the Kabbalah; by bringing together all the sciences, they try to accredit this maxim of to-day's philosophers, that man is the monkey of nature, a world in small, and that he creates forms and abstractions, as nature does matter and bodies; which leads to establishing that nature is the god of this world, and like a universal soul that puts everything in motion and action.

From the system of the Freemasons, of allowing all sects, of admitting all religions, it evidently follows that these gentlemen do not recognise any true one, and that the great Architect of the Universe, of whom they speak in terms so bombastic, is not really God. If indeed he was, how could he see with the same eye a Catholic and an anti-Trinitarian; a man who gives him attributes that the other denies him; a man who respected His word as the expression of His divine will, and a man who sees in it only the language of reason; a man who renders to Him the worship which He Himself has established, and another who renders Him none, who seeks, on the contrary, to prevent any being rendered to Him?

I know that many Masonic philosophers agree that there must be religion in the state; but is it not as if they were saying that all religions are indifferent in themselves, but that they are necessary to serve as barriers to the vices which human law cannot reach; that sensible people who know how to moderate their passions have no need of religion, but that one is necessary for the people who could not be restrained otherwise? These are the bases of philosophical tolerance, this is what the Freemasons want to establish, what enlightened people have seen, and what stopped them in the oath that was required of them.

True Christians do not fear equality, their religion teaches them to practice humility, which humbles them more than all the decrees of the Assembly can do; because it teaches them simplicity, modesty, self-abnegation. The Christian religion, by humbling all pride, by uprooting all ambition from the heart of man, by making all men brothers in *Jesus Christ*, by giving them the same father, the right to the same inheritance, has established true equality, and there is none comparable to it. It is also to this same religion that we owe true freedom, freedom of heart and passions, self-control, and the joy of a good conscience.

The Assembly elevates to the skies the freedom it offers us; but since it has made it present to us, in what sense have we become free? Insurgents have arisen in all the cities and even in the countryside, who subjugate opinions and seek to force the adoption of theirs. The most sacred secrets are no longer inviolable; the commerce of letters is not safe. One cannot travel without passports; often they are insufficient to deliver you from the hands of the malefactors one finds all along on the road.

For imaginary crimes you are confined in prisons, where you are subjected to shameful tortures. Liberty, if it exists, is for the wicked alone.

The advantages that the National Assembly has promised us, it has not procured for us; it has taken from us the goods we possessed; it demands along with the enemies of our Religion, oaths which we cannot swear. That we therefore repress the violence that is done to our conscience and to our faith, if it wants to see the French subjected to its decrees. That we do not find it wrong that pontiffs who can trace their succession back to the apostles, and through them, to *Jesus Christ*, refuse to recognise, as successors to the authority of *Jesus Christ*, the Scottish Masons who would like to steal their character with their mission. Now that the veil is lifted, I will reveal, if necessary, the iniquity hidden until now under the veil of the most inviolable secrecy. I am not a Mason; but I know their mysteries, and I will manifest them without fail in the faith of the oath.

THE END

Index